MARKET TIMING MODELS

Constructing, Implementing, & Optimizing a Market Timing–Based Investment Strategy

RICHARD ANDERSON

IRWIN
Professional Publishing©
Chicago • London • Singapore

◥▼ Times Mirror
M Higher Education Group

Library of Congress Cataloging-in-Publication Data
Anderson, Richard
    Market timing models : constructing, implementing, and optimizing a
market timing based investment strategy / Richard Anderson.
        p.   cm.
    Includes bibliographical references and index.
    ISBN 0-8763-1099-5
    1. Investment analysis—Mathematical models.   2. Speculation—
Mathematical models.   3. Stock price forecasting—Mathematical
models.   I. Title.
HG4529.A63   1997
332.6'01'51—dc20   96–20989

To Samuel Eisenstadt,
pioneer of quantitative investing.

PREFACE

Market timing, to be sure, is a controversial subject among those who participate in or otherwise observe the investment management scene. Indeed, there is no shortage of investment advisors who claim that timing the stock market will not outperform a buy-and-hold strategy.

My own experience is that market timing can, and does in practice, add value relative to a static, fully invested stance over time. Late in 1986 I began managing a market timing fund. In 1987, the year of the stock market crash, the fund outperformed U.S. equities, as measured by the Standard & Poor's 500, by about 10 percentage points. (I have long since moved on but the fund continues to do well, having outperformed the S&P 500 by about 5 percentage points annually from inception through 1995.)

Of course, 1987 was an extraordinary year in which there was no shortage of managers and advisors who did well relative to the market. For many, however, the fame was short-lived. Indeed, in the years from the October 1987 crash through the first half of the 1990s, market timing lost credibility. A persistent uptrend in the U.S. equity market in that period (broken only briefly in the second half of 1990) punished investors who underweighted stocks in their portfolios.

Despite the bad press some market timers have received in recent years, I know many practitioners have been quietly implementing market timing techniques successfully, and I think readers will find this book very helpful in explaining how forecasts can be used to enhance portfolio returns.

This book is perhaps the first regarding asset allocation to present detailed and broadly comprehensible descriptions of models designed to forecast financial markets. It has been written for virtually all readers with an interest in market timing. The econometrically inclined will find the underlying methods familiar, but other readers will be pleased to know that the text includes an introduction to the statistical techniques used to build the models.

Clearly there is more to managing a market timing investment program than just forecasting financial markets. Forecasts must be assessed for their reliability. The investor also must establish a level of tolerance for investment risk. Finally, the investor must synthesize a set of decision rules that incorporates forecasts and their reliability with the chosen level of risk tolerance. I address all of these "after-the-forecast-is-made" issues in this volume.

As an added bonus, I review the methodologies of three prominent Wall Street strategists. I chose Martin Zweig, Edward Kerschner, and Elaine Garzarelli for the diversity of their approaches as well their longstanding success as analysts.

As a result, I believe *Market Timing Models* will be of great interest to a broad array of readers. Clearly, it will interest both institutional and individual investors. But fiduciaries, such as pension managers and consultants, will find that coverage of the topic here offers insights regarding how to monitor investment managers who engage in market timing. Finally, academics and students of financial markets, finance in general, economics, and statistics will enjoy this book's treatment of applied forecasting techniques as they are used in the investment community.

ACKNOWLEDGMENTS

I am especially grateful to Richard Perline and Dan DiBartolomeo for their help in two disciplines central to this book, statistics and portfolio theory. In addition, I would like to thank Michael Carty, Robert Glickstein, Paul Graham, Louis Kirschbaum, Paul Lloyd, Lydia Miller, Sebastian Pugliese, Mark Tavel, and Eric Witkowski for their willingness to assist me in various ways. Of course, any shortcomings of this book are solely my responsibility.

CONTENTS

INTRODUCTION

MARKET TIMING DEFINED

Market timing is an investment strategy in which funds allocated to a designated set of assets are adjusted on an ongoing basis in response to changes in forecasts of return, volatility, or correlation of those assets. The designated set of assets could number as few as two (e.g., common stocks and cash equivalents) or include any subset of domestic and international stocks, bonds, and cash equivalents, as well as commodities and currencies. Allocation adjustments can occur from only rarely to as often as several times a month. Forecasts typically are generated on a methodical or ad hoc basis based on quantitative inputs, qualitative inputs, or both.

The size of the allocation adjustments can be a source of confusion. Some people define market timing as a process in which a manager periodically chooses the best performing asset among the designated set of assets and allocates 100 percent of a portfolio's funds to that asset. Since implementation of such a strategy can result in wide swings in performance, many see this type of market timer as a loose cannon on the investment scene.

The very term *market timing*, as a result, has taken on a bad connotation in some circles. Meanwhile, a newer term, **tactical asset allocation,** has filled the image gap for market timers. A manager who engages in tactical asset allocation typically makes relatively small changes to a fund's asset allocation in response to forecast changes. According to our definition of market timing, however, both managers engage in market timing inasmuch as they both adjust their portfolios in response to changing forecasts. The only difference between the "loose cannon" and the "tactical asset allocator" is that the loose cannon makes bigger bets in response to forecast changes.

Or so it may seem. Consider a pension fund with $100 million in assets. The fund hires a tactical asset allocator to make minor shifts in exposure to stocks in order to add value over a buy-and-hold stance. The board of directors has decided that, on a long-term basis, 60 percent of the fund should be invested in common stocks and 40 percent in bonds. The board authorizes the tactical asset allocator to let overall stock exposure range between 59 percent and 61 percent of the fund.

While it is true that this tactical asset allocator will make small bets relative to the $100 million fund, the bets relative to the funds the manager controls will be large. In this case, the board of directors might pass off $98 million to a manager with $59 million dedicated to stocks and $39 million to bonds. The remaining funds could go to the tactical asset allocator, who will have to make reasonably big bets relative to that $2 million under management in order to have an impact on the overall pension fund. In a sense then, tactical asset allocation can be reduced to something close to what some people call *market timing*. Hence, the broad definition. In this book, *market timing* and *tactical asset allocation* are used interchangeably.

Note the inclusion of forecasts of return, volatility, and correlation in our definition of market timing. Most people can imagine how return **forecasts** will drive the asset allocation process. When expected returns for stocks rise, a market timer probably would respond by increasing portfolio exposure to equities, assuming all other things are equal.

Volatility is a measure of the magnitude of price fluctuations, and therefore it is considered to be a measure of risk. Intuitively, if an asset becomes more volatile (risky) and expected returns remain the same, a market timer might respond by reducing exposure to that asset.

Correlation measures the tendency for asset prices to move together in the same or opposite direction. If one asset is highly correlated with another, a market timer might tend to substitute the one with the higher expected return for the other. Meanwhile, if two assets tend to move randomly relative to each other yet have equally positive expected returns, then a market timer might put both of them in a portfolio in roughly equal proportions, hoping that the random price fluctuations offset each other in a way that adds value to the portfolio. Adding value might mean reducing risk for a given level of return or increasing return for a given level of risk. The big prize goes to the portfolio manager who reduces risk and increases return.

Although return, volatility, and correlation go into the equation for determining asset allocation, it is probably true that changing forecasts of return dominate the process. Typically, but not always, volatility and correlation are determined by assumption, based on historical norms. As a result, volatility and correlation inputs tend to be stable, making changing return forecasts the key driver of the asset allocation process. One major exception is the possibility that a manager will use option prices to forecast future volatility. While such a strategy might add value, we will focus on forecasting return in order to meet the goal of adding value through market timing. In Chapter 11, we'll have the opportunity to confirm that returns are more important than volatility and correlation in determining optimal asset allocations.

THEY SAY IT CAN'T BE DONE

There is no question about it. The financial literature is stacked against market timing as a legitimate investment activity. One reason is that much of the financial research is written by academics who as a group have long held that markets are in one way or another "efficient." Broadly speaking, an efficient market incorporates all known information at all times, making it difficult to forecast future returns. Even if some small portion of the variation in future returns is predictable, moreover, the market efficiency crowd argues that implementation costs would eat up any potential gains from market timing.

Make no mistake: implementation costs can be significant. While commissions come to many peoples' minds, implementation costs also include the price of trading, that is, the difference between how much it costs to buy or sell an asset in a market at any given time. Investors "pay" half of the so-called **bid-ask spread** each time they trade. This observation can be shown by example. If a stock is trading at $18 bid–$20 asked, then buyers are paying $20 and sellers are receiving $18, making the true value of the stock $19. If this is the case, then a buyer or seller loses $1, or one-half the bid-ask spread on each trade. The trader's loss goes to the market maker, who takes the risk of holding an inventory of stock in order to maintain an orderly market.

Moreover, implementation costs can exceed the bid-ask spread. That's because investors who buy and sell assets in large quantities move prices away from their initial levels upon entry into the market. As a result, gains as a percent of assets under management will decline as the value of assets involved rises. At one extreme, an individual investor or small institutional portfolio manager with a modest level of information about future returns might be able to gain a few percentage points a year, which is not an insignificant figure considering that the average annual return on common stocks has been about 10 percent annually since the 1920s. At the other extreme, a well-managed market timing program will earn a tiny percentage of a large institutional account annually. But if the managers of a $20 billion pension fund add a mere two-tenths of a percent annually through a market timing program over a multiyear horizon, the 0.2 percent gain will be significant since it would reduce funding costs by $40 million a year.

Perhaps the most common argument against market timing dates back to the research of William Sharpe[1] in the mid 1970s in which he concluded that a manager needs a high level of forecast accuracy in order to achieve gains from market timing. The research put a hypothetical portfolio manager in the position of having to choose between stocks or Treasury bills at the beginning of each year from 1929 through 1972. The hypothetical portfolio was held unchanged until the next year when the manager was allowed to choose again between stocks and Treasury bills.

Based on these ground rules, Sharpe calculated that a portfolio manager with perfect foresight, that is, one who consistently picked stocks in the years that stocks outperformed Treasury bills and Treasury bills in the years when the reverse was true, would outperform a buy-and-hold strategy by about six percentage points annually. Obviously, no manager could have perfect foresight. Sharpe concluded that a manager needed to be more than 70 percent accurate in order for market timing to pay.

Nearly a decade after Sharpe's "Likely Gains from Stock Market Timing" appeared in the *Financial Analysts Journal*, Chua and Woodward[2] used largely the same ground rules for testing the plausibility that market timing can add value over a buy-and-hold strategy. They did investigate one important additional issue, however: What if a manager does a better job forecasting "bull market" years than "bear market" years? A manager with a 70 percent accuracy rate, for example, could be equally able to forecast bull and bear market years in the stock market. Alternatively, the manager could have had the same 70 percent overall accuracy by scoring 60 percent for bear markets and 80 percent for bull markets.

Chua and Woodward concluded that "forecasting accuracies necessary to achieve consistent positive gains are likely to be beyond the reach of most managers." This conclusion was based in part on the insights they gained by examining how market timing results fluctuated due to differential abilities in forecasting bull or bear years for the stock market. According to Chua and Woodward, correctly forecasting bull market years is more important than correctly forecasting bear market years. A buy-and-hold strategy will guarantee 100 percent forecast accuracy for bull market years and 0 percent forecast accuracy for bear market years (i.e, a buy-and-hold investor will participate in every bull market but will not avoid any bear markets). And, "since a less than perfect timing strategy lowers the accuracy of the more important result of hitting bull markets in favor of the less important result of avoiding bear markets, it should not be surprising that very high forecasting accuracies are necessary for timing to pay more than a buy-and-hold strategy."

Like many of the "it-can't-be-done" academic papers, the research cited above places an unrealistically severe constraint on the hypothetical market timer. In this case the restraint is the time between investment decisions. Recall that Sharpe concluded that the maximum gain from market timing, if a portfolio manager had perfect foresight, would be about six percentage points annually. Consider that nobody is perfect and subtract a little for implementation costs and it's hard to imagine anyone adding any value under those circumstances.

Consider now what happens if a portfolio manager is allowed to make a decision once a month instead of once a year. Under this new ground rule, perfect foresight can achieve an average annual return of about 36 percent a year versus about 9 percent for the buy-and-hold strategy over the years from 1929 through 1972, the period of Sharpe's initial study. How much forecast accuracy is required to capture even a small portion of that 27 percentage point spread? Not much, as it turns out. This result is explored in detail in Chapter 8.

Following up on the work of Fama and French,[3] Fuller and Kling[4] ask the question "Can Regression-Based Models Predict Stock and Bond Returns?" in the Spring 1994 issue of *The Journal of Portfolio Management*. Their answer is, "Not in a way that is useful to practitioners."

The Fuller and Kling study, which covers the period from 1926 through 1988, tests whether certain factors can forecast stock and bond market returns. The predictive factors tested, dividend yields, the term premium, and the default premium were introduced in the earlier Fama and French article. The **term premium** was defined as the difference between the yield on high-quality corporate bonds and the one-month Treasury bill yield. The **default premium** was defined as the difference in yield between a bond portfolio of average quality and one of high quality.

The empirical results show that dividend yields and default premiums tend to be good longer-term (i.e., three to four years) predictors of stock and bond market returns. Meanwhile, the term premium, which is more closely related to the shorter-term business cycle, tends to be a better predictor of horizons from one month to two years. Despite the apparent usefulness in a statistical sense of the variables considered, Fuller and Kling concluded that they do not have enough explanatory power to benefit an investor trying to time the stock and bond markets, especially when transaction costs are considered.

Without going into details, it's fair to say that the Fuller and Kling article is relatively straightforward in terms of the statistical tests they used on the data to reach their conclusion. There is something very troubling about the logic of the title of their article, however. Essentially they said, "We tested a few regression-based models. They didn't work. Therefore, no regression-based models can predict stock and bond market returns in a way that is useful to practitioners." In Chapters 4 through 7 we will review several models that are likely to add value in a way that is useful to practitioners. I know, because I've seen such models add value in real time over the past 10 years.

AN OVERVIEW OF THIS BOOK

It's probably no surprise that a book called *Market Timing Models* is going argue that market timing can add value to an investment program. The first section of this book explores some rudimentary models in order to present the basics of regression analysis. This material is by no means meant to be comprehensive, however, and the uninitiated who develop an interest in regression-based forecasting models are advised to refer to a textbook on econometrics. A few are cited throughout this volume.

Section 2 presents four regression-based models, one each for stocks, bonds, the relative performance of small- and large-capitalization stocks, and the Canadian dollar. All variables used for forecasting are fully disclosed and background information on the evolution of the models is included.

Section 3 addresses the real-world problem of how to use model forecasts. In Chapter 8, using the stock market as an example, we explore how much explanatory power a model has to have to add value. Three different trading rules for managing a market timing portfolio are introduced. In Chapter 9, we simulate the use of the models introduced in Section 2. Special emphasis is placed on how simulations or "back tests" can fool an investor into believing a model is worth more than it really is. Chapter 10 covers the issue of translating model forecasts into investment decisions. We start with certain naive but nevertheless effective strategies and culminate with the construction of a spreadsheet that calculates optimal portfolio allocations given a set of forecasts. Here we learn that some of the simple asset allocation rules discussed earlier are indeed efficient, according to modern portfolio theory.

Chapter 11 reviews three other approaches to market timing—that of Martin Zweig, Edward Kerschner, and Elaine Garzarelli. Each strategist has an enviable track record and a unique method of forecasting financial markets. Some readers may find an intriguing challenge in trying to design a superior market timing process that borrows from any or all of the ideas reviewed in this book. Designing your own process and other ideas for improving market timing investment programs appear in the final chapter of concluding remarks.

Appendix 1 offers a quick overview of the mechanics of a regression model. Appendix 2 provides the data set used for the rudimentary models discussed in Section 1. Appendix 3 lists sources for data and asset allocation and statistical software. A glossary of terms, endnotes, and an index appear at the end of the text.

A final note: Readers who wish to receive ongoing forecasts and research updates may write: Market Timing Models, Attn: Richard Anderson, 2930 Courtside Drive, Roseville, CA 95661. The e-mail adress is mtmodels@aol.com.

I

INTRODUCTION TO REGRESSION ANALYSIS

1

FORECASTING THE STOCK MARKET USING A SINGLE PREDICTOR VARIABLE

A SIMPLE MODEL

We'll start by looking at a model designed to forecast the annual total return on the stock market, that is, the return that includes both price changes and dividends, using a single **predictor variable:** the **dividend yield.**

Table 1–1 shows the yearend dividend yield on the S&P 500 and the total return on the S&P 500 in the next year for the period 1938 through 1991. As an example, we will try to predict the return on the stock market in 1979 based on the dividend yield on the market at the end of 1978.

The stock market's dividend yield is considered an indicator of value. When it is low, an investor does not get much dividend income for each dollar invested in equities, which suggests that stocks are expensive and that the return over the next year might well be below average. Conversely, when the dividend yield is high, stocks are considered to be cheap, which indicates the possibility of an above-average return on the market in the

TABLE 1-1

Yearend Dividend Yield on the S&P 500 versus the Total Return on the S&P 500 in the Following Year

Year	Yield at Yearend	Subsequent Year's Return	Year	Yield at Yearend	Subsequent Year's Return	Year	Yield at Yearend	Subsequent Year's Return
1938	3.58%	-0.4%	1956	4.24%	-10.8%	1974	5.43%	37.2%
1939	4.54	-9.8	1957	4.64	43.4	1975	4.14	23.8
1940	6.37	-11.6	1958	3.33	12.0	1976	3.93	-7.2
1941	8.13	20.3	1959	3.18	0.5	1977	5.11	6.6
1942	5.84	25.9	1960	3.41	26.9	1978	5.42	18.4
1943	5.07	19.8	1961	2.85	-8.7	1979	5.53	32.4
1944	4.77	36.4	1962	3.40	22.8	1980	4.74	-4.9
1945	3.71	-8.1	1963	3.13	16.5	1981	5.57	21.4
1946	4.47	5.7	1964	3.05	12.5	1982	4.93	22.5
1947	5.55	5.5	1965	3.05	-10.1	1983	4.32	6.3
1948	6.24	18.8	1966	3.59	24.0	1984	4.68	32.2
1949	6.75	31.7	1967	3.09	11.1	1985	3.88	18.5
1950	7.24	24.0	1968	2.93	-8.5	1986	3.38	5.2
1951	5.99	18.4	1969	3.52	4.0	1987	3.71	16.8
1952	5.47	-1.0	1970	3.46	14.3	1988	3.68	31.5
1953	5.83	52.6	1971	3.10	19.0	1889	3.33	-3.2
1954	4.45	31.6	1972	2.70	-14.7	1990	3.74	30.6
1955	4.15	6.6	1973	3.70	-26.5	1991	3.11	7.7

Sources: © Stocks, Bonds, Bills, and Inflation 1996 Yearbook™, Ibbotson Associates, Chicago (annually updates work by Roger G. Ibbotson and Rex A. Sinquefield). Used with permission. All rights reserved. Standard & Poor's. Used by permission of Standard & Poor's, a division of the McGraw-Hill Companies.

next year. That's the essence of this one-variable model designed to forecast the return on the stock market each year.

To test the idea of this model, Table 1–2 presents the dividend yield and return data a bit differently. In this table, data are sorted by dividend yield rather than chronologically. The first entry shows the yearend with the lowest dividend yield and return on the stock market in the following year. The last entry shows the yearend with the highest dividend yield and the return on the market in the next year. Also shown is the average total return for each of the three columns of data.

The summary data at the bottom of Table 1–2 for the three groups of returns are encouraging. The group with the lowest dividend yields had an average total return of only 6.0 percent. The average total return for the high dividend yield group, however, amounted to a whopping 21.1 percent. The average for the middle column was 11.3 percent, in between the other two. Thus Table 1–2 supports the idea of the model: Low dividend yields are followed by lower returns, on average, and high dividend yields are generally followed by above-average returns.

We have to treat any inferences from this result with caution. That's because we have the benefit of knowing exactly which dividend yields comprised the bottom, middle, and top third of the range from 1938 through 1991. Obviously, however, if we had started investing in 1938, we could not have known that selling shares when the dividend yield was less than 3.6 percent and mortgaging the house to buy stocks when the dividend yield was greater than 4.7 percent would have yielded a superior return. The simple truism that hindsight is 20–20 is a most important concept that cannot be overemphasized when working with statistically based investment processes.

When a trading rule is tested based on pure hindsight, there is really no forecasting involved. Such a test is based on **in-sample forecasts.** In the case above, the sample is the 54 years of yearend dividend yields and subsequent year stock

TABLE 1-2

Yearend Dividend Yield on the S&P 500 versus the Total Return on the S&P 500 in the Following Year*

Year	Yield at Yearend	Subsequent Year's Return	Year	Yield at Yearend	Subsequent Year's Return	Year	Yield at Yearend	Subsequent Year's Return
1972	2.70%	-14.7%	1966	3.59%	24.0%	1944	4.77%	36.4%
1961	2.85	-8.7	1988	3.68	31.5	1982	4.93	22.5
1968	2.93	-8.5	1973	3.70	-26.5	1943	5.07	19.8
1964	3.05	12.5	1945	3.71	-8.1	1977	5.11	6.6
1965	3.05	-10.1	1987	3.71	16.8	1978	5.42	18.4
1967	3.09	11.1	1990	3.74	30.6	1974	5.43	37.2
1971	3.10	19.0	1985	3.88	18.5	1952	5.47	-1.0
1991	3.11	9.0	1976	3.93	-7.2	1979	5.53	32.4
1963	3.13	16.5	1975	4.14	23.8	1947	5.55	5.5
1959	3.18	0.5	1955	4.15	6.6	1981	5.57	21.4
1958	3.33	12.0	1956	4.24	-10.8	1953	5.83	52.6
1989	3.33	-3.2	1983	4.32	6.3	1942	5.84	25.9
1986	3.38	5.2	1954	4.45	31.6	1951	5.99	18.4
1962	3.40	22.8	1946	4.47	5.7	1948	6.24	18.8
1960	3.41	26.9	1939	4.54	-9.8	1940	6.37	-11.6
1970	3.46	14.3	1957	4.64	43.4	1949	6.75	31.7
1969	3.52	4.0	1984	4.68	32.2	1950	7.24	24.0
1938	3.58	-0.4	1980	4.74	-4.9	1941	8.13	20.3
Averages		6.0%			11.3%			21.1

*Observations are sorted by divicend yield.

Sources: © Stocks, Bonds, Bills, and Inflation 1996 Yearbook™, Ibbotson Associates, Chicago (annually updates work by Roger G. Ibbotson and Rex A. Sinquefield). Used with permission. All rights reserved. Standard & Poor's. Used by permission of Standard & Poor's, a division of the McGraw-Hill Companies.

returns. The test is "in" sample because the rule was constructed and tested using the same data set.

When a forecast is made for a period outside of the estimation period, it is called an **out-of-sample forecast.** There are two types of out-of-sample forecasts. If it is 1999 and we use the data from 1938 through 1991 to create a forecast for 1992, then this out-of-sample forecast is called an **ex post forecast**—ex post is short for *ex post facto* or *after the fact* in Latin—because in 1999 the 1992 result has already occurred. If, however, a researcher in 1999 uses data through 1999 to make a forecast for the year 2000, the forecast is called **ex ante** (*ex ante facto* means before the fact) because the outcome is not known at the time of the forecast.

Arguably one of the most important points regarding tests of statistical models is that they should be out-of-sample rather than in-sample. In order to test or simulate a model's effectiveness over an extended period, the out-of-sample test must be ex post. Once a model is thoroughly tested and is being used to forecast one period ahead in real time, the out-of-sample forecasts become ex ante forecasts.

Now let's suppose it is 1992 and we want to forecast the total return on the stock market using the yearend dividend yield as the predictor variable. Establishing a forecast based on the data in Table 1–2 would be cumbersome, at best. Based on the way the data is organized, a forecast rule would be limited to something like this: When the dividend yield falls below 3.60 percent, expect a limited return on the stock market, on average; when the dividend yield rises above 4.75 percent, however, look for an above-average return. But given a specific dividend yield, we would not be able to establish a specific forecast based solely on these guidelines.

Estimating the reliability of a forecast based on the data in Table 1–2 would be difficult as well. Upon examining the low dividend group (average return: 6 percent), about the best that could be said is that the highest return in that group was 26.9 percent (20.9 percentage points above the average) and that the

FIGURE 1–1

Dividend Yield versus Stock Returns, 1938–1991

The total return on the stock market is plotted against the dividend yield in this chart. The cloud of points tends to move up from left to right, indicating a positive relationship between dividend yields and stock returns. That is, when dividend yields are low, subsequent stock returns tend to be below average. Higher dividend yields are generally followed by above-average stock returns.

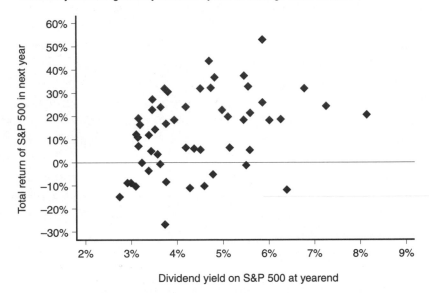

Dividend yield on S&P 500 at yearend

Source: © *Stocks, Bonds, Bills, and Inflation 1996 Yearbook™*, Ibbotson Associates, Chicago (annually updates work by Roger G. Ibbotson and Rex A. Sinquefield). Used with permission. All rights reserved. Standard & Poor's. Used by permission of Standard & Poor's, a division of the McGraw-Hill Companies.

lowest return was –14.7 percent (20.7 percentage points below the average).

THE LINEAR REGRESSION MODEL

Fortunately, a relatively simple statistical technique called **regression** analysis, or **linear regression,** not only provides specific forecasts, but also offers an indicator of forecast reliability. The idea behind regression can be illustrated graphically. Figure 1–1 is a plot of the dividend yield and return data previously presented in Tables 1–1 and 1–2. Each point in the chart represents a dividend yield at the end of one year and the return on the market in the following year. By convention, the returns (what we are trying to predict) are measured along the vertical axis. The dividend yield (the predictor variable) is measured along the horizontal axis. Notice that the cloud of points rises from left to right. This is consistent with our previous observation that stock market returns tend to be higher when dividend yields are higher.

The same data is plotted in Figure 1–2 with the so-called regression line through the cloud of points. To understand how the regression line was drawn, consider one of the points in Figure 1–2. Imagine the vertical distance between that point and the regression line. Now imagine squaring that vertical distance, that is, multiplying the distance by itself. Finally, consider all of the squared vertical distances between the points and the line. Add them up. The regression line is the unique line that minimizes the sum of those squared differences. Using this minimization as the criteria, this **least squares** regression line offers a "best" linear fit for the data.

REGRESSION AND LEAST SQUARES: SOME BACKGROUND

The term *regression* dates back to the work of the English scientist Francis Galton, who in 1875 began some hereditary experiments with sweet peas. Galton asked seven friends to grow 70 sweet pea plants. Each friend received a packet of 70 seeds divided into seven categories by weight, with 10 seeds for each category.

In examining the weight of the seeds produced by the sweet pea plants, Galton observed that the progeny seeds did not have the same average weight as the parent seeds. Rather, in all cases, the average weight of the progeny seeds was between the weight of the parent average and the average of all seven parent groups. Galton called this tendency *reversion*, and it later became known as *regression to the mean*.

F I G U R E 1–2

Dividend Yield versus Stock Returns, 1938–1991

The regression line is included in this plot of the total return on the stock market versus the dividend yield. The regression line represents the best straight-line fit of the relationship between stock market returns and dividend yields. The regression line is the unique line that minimizes the squared vertical distances *d* between it and the points on the chart.

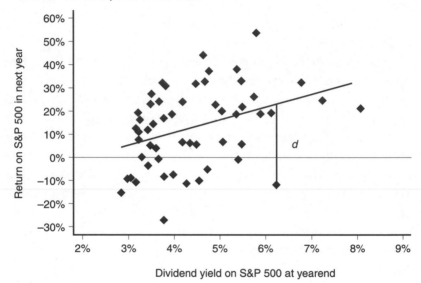

Dividend yield on S&P 500 at yearend

Galton also observed that the sweet pea regression was linear: the difference between the average offspring weight and the overall parent population average was consistently only one-third as great as the comparable parental differential. In symbols,

$$W_{Off} = W_{Pop} + 1/3 \times (W_{Par} - W_{Pop})$$

where

W_{Off} = Average weight of an offspring group.

W_{Pop} = Average weight of the overall parent population.

W_{Par} = Average weight of the parent group.

Based on this linear relationship, Galton could estimate or forecast average offspring weights based on the parental and overall population averages. Later we will see that our market timing forecasts will be based exactly on the same type of linear relationship.

Nearly a century before Galton was sowing the seeds of linear regression, the least squares method was developed as a consequence of an entirely different inquiry. At the time, the European scientific community was investigating the paths of the moon and certain planets by making successive observations of their positions. Due to errors in measurement, the points, when plotted, did not form a smooth curve. So from well into the 18th century to the beginning of the 19th, considerable work was done on the so-called theory of errors. The objective was to find the curve, based on the plot of the repeated observations, that best represented the true path of a celestial body such as the moon.

In 1805, the French mathematician A.M. Legendre proposed the least squares technique to estimate the curves, and it is fair to say that Legendre's suggestion was an instant hit. The new method was simple and had intuitive appeal. Indeed, it appears that the great mathematician Carl Friedrich Gauss had been using the least squares technique for 10 years before Legendre proposed it.

Although Legendre probably deserves credit for first proposing the least squares technique—certainly he was the first to describe it in print—Gauss concluded just four years later, in 1809, that under certain theoretical conditions, least squares provided the best estimate of the path of a celestial object. Though his initial proof was a little shaky, his intuition turned out to be on the mark. Thus, not only was the least squares technique intuitively attractive, but also it was theoretically justified as the best solution for a wide variety of problems.

Gauss's key assumption was that the measurement errors had a **normal distribution.** That is, a plot showing the distribution of the errors would look like the well-known bell curve. If this condition held, then least squares turned out to be the best estimator of the true path of a celestial body, given a series of observations of its position.[5]

THE CLASSICAL LINEAR REGRESSION MODEL

The normality assumption evolved over the next century or so into what are called *assumptions of the classical linear regression model,* or **classical assumptions.** In brief, they are:

1. The relationship between the **forecast variable** and the predictor variable[6] is linear, that is, it can be described by a straight line.

2. Each predictor variable value can be selected by the researcher. If not, then there is no relationship between the predictor variables and the error terms.

3. The error term, on average, is zero. The magnitude of the error term fluctuations about the zero mean is constant.

4. There is no relationship between successive error terms; in other words, the error terms are not "serially correlated."

5. The error terms are normally distributed—if plotted, the distribution of errors would resemble the bell curve.

If assumptions 1–4 hold, then the least squares technique will produce the best possible linear estimate of the relationship between the forecast and predictor variables. If assumption 5 holds as well, then certain statistical tests will provide assessments of the accuracy of the regression estimates.

Oftentimes we will find that not all of the classical assumptions will be satisfied. For example, although some medical or social researchers can control the values of their predictor variables experimentally, this assumption does not hold true for economic analysis. Obviously, a financial analyst cannot control the dividend yield in our stock market example. Meanwhile, it is virtually impossible to show that a predictor variable is or is not correlated to the error terms. So analysts who model financial markets typically ignore assumption number 2. If any of the other four assumptions are violated, sometimes the discrepancy will be ignored; other times, an offsetting action will be taken.

Despite potential violations of the classical linear model assumptions, regression analysis is a very hardy process. That is, departures from the assumptions typically will not diminish the accuracy of regression estimates and forecasts. In sum, regression analysis is relatively simple, intuitively reasonable, and robust with respect to violations of its classical assumptions. Hence, it is used in this volume.

The least squares method does have at least one inconvenient drawback. When the distances are squared a large penalty is placed on points far away from the line. A point one unit away from the regression line has a squared distance of one, while a point five units away has a squared distance of 25. This property puts more emphasis on faraway points, called **outliers,** in a way that can distort the regression line.

Another thought regarding the "best" fit: Why should the regression line be a straight line? Why not a curved line? The answer is that experience indicates a curved line probably would not improve the forecast. Consider that unruly cloud of points in Figure 1–1. Perhaps a curved line exists that fits the data better. Given the messy data and little theory to justify a curved line, however, any improvement in the fit probably would be limited to data in question. That is, a nonlinear model might look better than the linear model for the period from 1938 through 1991, but its forecasts might well be inferior from 1992 through the year 2000 and beyond.

CREATING FORECASTS AND INTERPRETING
REGRESSION OUTPUT

A regression forecast can be visualized by taking another look at Figure 1–2. Suppose it's New Year's Eve. The dividend yield on the **S&P 500** is 5 percent. In order to find the model's forecast, find 5 percent on the horizontal axis. From there, go straight up to the regression line and then look across to the vertical axis to find what looks like about 15 percent. Thus, given a 5 percent dividend yield, the model forecasts approximately a 15 percent return on the stock market in the year ahead.

The model's exact forecast can be determined with the help of the regression output, which was obtained from a standard regression software package, shown in Table 1–3. Two numbers in the table define the regression line. The constant indicates where the regression line, if extended to the left, would intersect with the vertical axis of total return, the Y-intercept. The **X-coefficient** indicates how steep the regression line is and whether the line is going uphill or downhill. The larger the X-coefficient, the steeper the line—a regression line going downhill would have a negative X-coefficient. The exact forecast is determined by multiplying the X-coefficient by the dividend yield and adding that product to the constant. Given that the constant is –0.09, the X-coefficient is 4.89 and a dividend yield of 5 percent (or 0.05), the exact forecast is:

$$-0.09 + (4.89 \times 0.05) = .15 = 15\%$$

That is, given a dividend yield of 5 percent in December, the forecast for the return on the stock market in the following year is 15 percent.

What about the other numbers that appear in the regression output in Table 1–3? The standard error of Y estimate is a measure of how far, on average, the points are from the regression line in Figure 1–2. The regression output in Table 1–3 indicates a standard error of Y estimate of .16, or 16 percent. Using

T A B L E   1–3

Regression Output for a Model with a Single Predictor Variable
(dividend yield)*

Constant	−0.09
Standard error of Y estimate	0.16
R-squared	0.13
Number of observations	54
X-coefficient	4.91
Standard error of X-coefficient	1.75
T-statistic	2.81

*This model forecasts the annual total return on the stock market. The estimation period is 1938–1991.

Sources: Y: © *Stocks, Bonds, Bills, and Inflation 1996 Yearbook™*, Ibbotson Associates, Chicago (annually updates work by Roger G. Ibbotson and Rex A. Sinquefield). Used with permission. All rights reserved.

X: Standard & Poor's. Used with permission of Standard & Poor's, a division of the McGraw-Hill Companies.

some basic assumptions from statistical theory, given a model forecast, there is approximately a 68 percent probability that the actual return will differ from the forecast by no more than one standard error of Y estimate and about a 95 percent probability that it will differ by no more than twice the standard error of Y estimate. Recall that given a 5 percent dividend yield, the forecast of the return on the stock market was 15 percent. The standard error of Y estimate for the model indicates there is approximately a 95 percent probability that the actual return on the stock market will be:

$$\text{Forecast} \pm 2 \times (\text{Standard Error of } Y \text{ Estimate}) =$$
$$15\% \pm (2 \times 16\%)$$

That is, there is approximately a 95 percent probability that the actual return will fall between −17 percent (15% − (2 × 16%)) and 47 percent (15% + (2 × 16%)).

Admittedly, we could drive a truck through the 95 percent confidence interval for the model's forecast. Happily, a more accurate stock market timing model will be introduced in Chapter 4.

For purposes of introducing the vocabulary of regression analysis, however, we will continue to use simpler models in the first three chapters of this book.

The **R-squared** (.13 or 13 percent in the regression output in Table 1–3) indicates how much of the squared variation in the variable being predicted (the return on the stock market in the current example) is explained by the regression model. This concept needs some explanation. The R-squared is also called the coefficient of determination.

The idea is first to make a best guess for Y without the benefit of an explanatory variable. The best guess is the average of Y (the sum of all Ys divided by the number of Ys). The next step is to take the difference between each value of Y and the average, and then square that difference. The sum of the squared differences represents a sort of cumulative measure of error that we would make if, in trying to estimate each value of Y, we used the average of Y as a guess. This sum is called the total sum of squares of Y from its mean.

Now suppose we have a predictor variable that can be used to create a regression line. If we take the sum of the squared vertical distances between each point and the regression line (the squares of the error terms), we have a measure of what is left unexplained by the model. This sum is sometimes called the residual sum of squares. It is a mathematical theorem that unexplained squared variation plus explained squared variation equals total squared variation. This means that in order to find the explained squared variation, all we have to do is subtract the unexplained squared variation from the total squared variation. That is, if

$$\text{Explained} + \text{Unexplained} = \text{Total}$$

then

$$\text{Explained} = \text{Total} - \text{Unexplained}$$

The R-squared is calculated by dividing the explained squared variation by the total squared variation (see Figure 1–3).

FIGURE 1–3

Measuring the R-Squared

In the first chart the average value of Y is used as an estimate of Y. The horizontal line represents that average. The total sum of squared variation T is calculated by squaring the vertical distance d between each point and the horizontal line and adding up the squared distances. The same calculation is done against the regression line in the second chart. The second sum is the squared variation left unexplained U by the regression. The squared variation explained by the regression E is the total squared variation less the unexplained squared variation, that is, $E = T - U$. The R-squared for the regression equals the ratio between the explained squared variation and the total squared variation, or E/T.

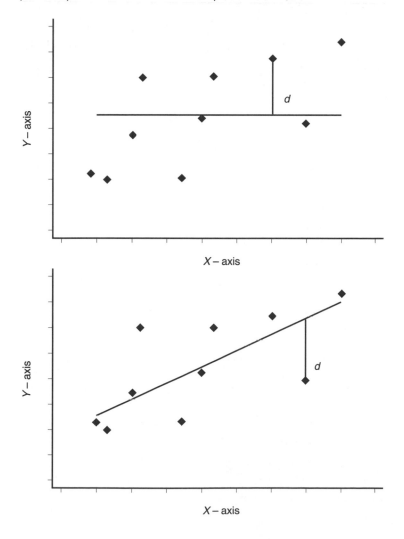

The *R*-squared for our one-variable stock market model tells us that the model explains 13 percent of the squared variation in annual stock market returns. In general, given two models, the one with the higher *R*-squared would be considered a better model because it explains more of the squared variation of the variable the model is trying to predict.

The number of observations shown Table 1–3 is 54. In our model, each year is an observation, and there are 54 of them from 1938 through 1991.

The standard error of the *X*-coefficient is 1.75. The standard error of the coefficient indicates that there is approximately a 95 percent probability that the actual *X*-coefficient is

$$X-\text{Coefficient} \pm 2 \times (\text{Standard Error of } X\text{-Coefficient}) =$$
$$4.89 \pm 2 \times 1.75$$

That is, there is approximately a 95 percent probability that the actual value of the *X*-coefficient is between 1.39 (4.89 – (2 × 1.75)) and 8.39 (4.89 + (2 × 1.75)).

The **t-statistic** is calculated by dividing the *X*-coefficient by the standard error of the *X*-coefficient. Generally, when a *t*-statistic is greater than 2 or less than –2, then there is at least a 95 percent probability that the *X*-coefficient does not equal zero. The *t*-statistic for the *X*-coefficient is 2.79, according to Table 1–3, indicating a very high probability that the *X*-coefficient does not equal zero.

Why does it matter that the *X*-coefficient might equal zero? Recall that the model's forecast was calculated as follows:

$$\text{Forecast} = \text{Constant} + (X\text{-Coefficient} \times \text{Dividend Yield})$$

If the *X*-coefficient were zero, then the forecast would not change, no matter what the dividend yield was. In other words, if the *X*-coefficient were zero, the dividend yield would not be a useful predictor of stock market returns, and it would not belong in a regression model designed to forecast the stock market.

2

FORECASTING THE STOCK MARKET USING SEVERAL PREDICTOR VARIABLES

In Chapter 1 we used a single variable, the dividend yield, to predict stock market returns. The statistical technique used, regression analysis, modeled the relationship between the predictor variable (dividend yield) and the forecast variable (stock market returns). Now we want to add another variable to enhance the explanatory power of our model.

ADDING A SECOND VARIABLE TO A MODEL

One potential candidate for a second predictor variable is the price-earnings ratio. Like the dividend yield, the **price-earnings (PE) ratio** is considered an indicator of value. When the PE ratio is high, investors are paying top dollar for each unit of earnings, making stocks expensive and the likelihood of above-average performance low. Likewise, when the PE ratio is low, stocks are cheap, making above-average performance more likely. Of course, an elevated PE ratio often reflects investor anticipation of strong earnings growth. As with virtually all financial mar-kets, however, investor anticipation often exceeds subsequent reality, making the PE ratio a good contrary indicator.

How might we add the market PE ratio to our model? One way would be to redo the analysis in Chapter 1 with the PE ratio in the place of the dividend yield. Then we could have two sep-arate models—one using the dividend yield and the other using the price-earnings ratio—to predict stock market returns. An average of the two models' forecasts might offer an improve-ment over either of the models used separately. Better yet, we could consider weighting the forecasts according to the explana-tory power of each model, putting more weight on the forecast from the model with the higher R-squared.

It's not difficult to imagine varying the weights assigned to each model in a methodical manner to find the best combina-tion. Although tedious, a pretty good solution could be found, especially with the help of a personal computer. If a third pre-dictor variable is added, however, the number of combinations of weights to test rises exponentially. Add a few more predictor variables and the problem becomes unmanageable.

Fortunately, such a process is not necessary, since regression analysis can handle more than one predictor variable. If a sec-ond predictor variable is added, regression analysis will produce not one, but two X-coefficients. How might they be interpreted?

Recall that in the regression with one predictor variable the forecast was calculated as follows:

$$\text{Forecast} = \text{Constant} + (X\text{-Coefficient}) \times (X\text{-Variable})$$

Using two predictor variables the forecast is calculated as:

$$\text{Forecast} = \text{Constant} + (X\text{-Coef \#1}) \times (X\text{-Var \#1}) \\ + (X\text{-Coef \#2}) \times (X\text{-Var \#2})$$

In order to save a little space, the equation can be written like this:

$$\text{Forecast} = C_0 + C_1 X_1 + C_2 X_2$$

where

C_0 = Constant.
C_1 = Coefficient of the first X variable.
X_1 = The first X variable.
C_2 = Coefficient of the second X variable.
X_2 = The second X variable.

The interpretation of the two X-coefficients in the two–predictor variable regression is an extension of the interpretation of the X-coefficient in the one–predictor variable regression. Consider the equation for the two–predictor variable regression forecast once again:

$$\text{Forecast} = C_0 + C_1 X_1 + C_2 X_2$$

The constant C_0 tells us what the forecast would be if both X_1 and X_2 equal zero. The coefficient C_1 tells us how much the forecast will change if X_1 changes by one unit, assuming that X_2 is held constant. Likewise, the coefficient C_2 indicates the impact of a one-unit change in X_2, assuming X_1 is held constant.

LOOKING FOR ADDITIONAL PREDICTOR VARIABLES

Now that we know we can use more than one predictor variable in a regression model, how might we go about finding other variables to consider adding to the model developed in Chapter 1? One way is to test each potential predictor variable separately in a regression model against stock returns. Variables with high R-squareds might well be promising additions to the model.

Many analysts find it useful to look at a statistic related to, but slightly different than, the R-squared measure. Consider the square root of the R-squared. If the forecast and predictor variables rise and fall together, put a plus sign in front of the figure, indicating positive comovement between the variables. If the forecast variable moves down when the predictor variable moves up, put a minus sign (indicating negative comovement) in front of the figure.

We now have a measure that can take on values from –1 to +1. A value of +1 indicates perfectly linear positive comovement between the predictor variable and the forecast variable. In a graph with the forecast variable on the Y-axis and the predictor variable on the X-axis, as in Figure 2–1, the points would form a straight line running uphill. If the predictor variable is known, then the forecast variable can be predicted with perfect accuracy. Similarly, a value of –1 would indicate perfectly negative linear comovement. The points would fall on a straight line going downhill. Knowledge of the predictor variable means that the forecast variable can be calculated with certainty. Finally, if the measure of comovement turns out to be 0, then there is no linear relationship between the predictor and forecast variables.

The measure of comovement described above is called the *correlation coefficient.* Let's look at correlation coefficients between some new potential predictor variables and stock market returns. Perhaps we can find a promising new predictor variable to add to the regression model using the dividend yield developed in Chapter 1.

Table 2–1 shows correlations between potential predictor variables and stock market returns for the years from 1942 through 1992. The first group of variables includes the dividend yield (already discussed) and interest rates. Broadly speaking, rising interest rates are associated with declining stock prices; declining rates, with rising stock prices. Also included are variables related to earnings (which affect a company's ability to pay dividends), variables related to inflation (considered a negative influence on stock prices); and the past performance of the stock market itself.

The final group of variables in Table 2–1 lists some of the variables a second time in a different form: the change in the variable over the past year, in contrast to the current level of the

FIGURE 2–1

Examples of Linear Relationships

Three charts showing perfectly positive, perfectly negative, and no linear relationship between predictor and forecast variables.

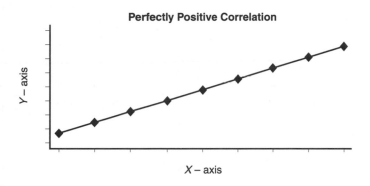

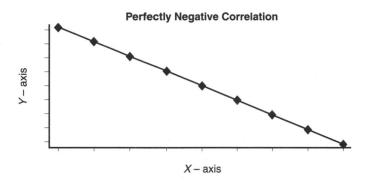

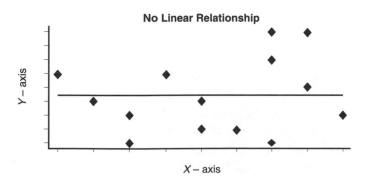

TABLE 2–1

Correlation Coefficients between Potential Predictor Variables and Annual
Stock Market Returns (1942–1992)

Variable	Correlation
Dividend yield	0.43
T-bill yield	−0.02
Aaa bond yield	−0.01
Baa bond yield	0.01
Baa yield less Aaa yield	0.14
Price-earnings ratio	−0.38
Earnings yield (1/(PE ratio))	0.37
Earnings	0.02
Gross domestic product deflator	0.02
Consumer price inflation	0.02
Stock market return—past year	−0.15
Stock market return—past two years	−0.27
One-year change in dividend yield	0.11
One-year change in T-bill yield	−0.09
One-year change in earnings	−0.09
One-year change in Aaa yield	0.10
One-year change in Baa yield	0.16
One-year change in (Baa-Aaa yields)	0.24

Sources: Standard & Poor's. Used with permission of Standard & Poor's, a division of the McGraw-Hill Companies. © *Stocks, Bonds, Bills, and Inflation Yearbook™*, Ibbotson Associates, Chicago (annually updates work by Roger G. Ibbotson and Rex A. Sinquefield). Used with permission. All rights reserved. Used with permission of Moody's Investor's Service; U.S. Dept. of Commerce; U.S. Department of Labor.

variable. The issue of whether to use the level of variable, a measure of change over a period of time, or even a measure of
"change in change" is an important one. In physical terms the
level of a variable can be likened to the position of a car on a
highway; change in a variable, to the car's velocity; and change
in change, to the car's acceleration. It is often a good idea to test
all three forms when exploring the potential value of a predictor

variable. We'll discuss the three basic forms of variables more in Chapter 3.

Notice that the dividend yield, with a correlation of 0.43, has the highest correlation of the variables listed in the table. The next best variable is the price-earnings ratio, followed by its reciprocal, the earnings yield. Since the information in these two variables is largely the same, the absolute value of the correlations is nearly equal, but the signs are opposite. Thus, a high price relative to earnings, or a high PE ratio, is negatively correlated with future stock returns. The flip side is that high earnings relative to price, or a high **earnings-price (EP) ratio,** is positively correlated with future stock returns. The only difference in the information in the two is that one variable equals 1 divided by the other, that is,

$$PE = 1 \; / \; (EP).$$

So at this point we probably would be indifferent to using PE versus EP. But it is conceivable that under certain circumstances one form would be preferred over the other on theoretical grounds. And of course we can always test the question empirically, that is, look at the historical record to see which form actually has been the better predictor variable.

REGRESSION RESULTS FOR SOME NEW MODELS

Now let's see if we can improve our model by adding a second predictor variable to the regression. What we will do is run our old friend, the one–predictor variable model using dividend yield. Then we'll look at the PE ratio as a single predictor variable. Finally, we'll run a third regression: one with the dividend yield and the PE ratio together.

The results for the three regression models are shown in Table 2–2. Let's consider the results for the model that includes the dividend yield and the PE ratio. The regression output shows no improvement in the R-squared. For the model with

T A B L E   2–2

Regression Output for Three Models (1942–1992)

(1) Stock Market Returns versus Dividend Yield	
Constant	−0.11
Standard error of *Y* estimate	0.15
R-squared	0.19
Number of observations	51
	Dividend Yield
X-coefficient	5.77
Standard error of *X*-coefficient	1.71
T-statistic	3.37

(2) Stock Market Returns versus PE Ratio	
Constant	0.34
Standard error of *Y* estimate	0.15
R-squared	0.14
Number of observations	51
	PE Ratio
X-coefficient	−0.015
Standard error of *X*-coefficient	0.005
T-statistic	−2.881

(3) Stock Market Returns versus Dividend Yield and PE Ratio		
Constant	−0.07	
Standard error of *Y* estimate	0.15	
R-squared	0.19	
Number of observations	51	
	Dividend Yield	**PE Ratio**
X-coefficient	5.26	−0.002
Standard error of *X*-coefficient	3.27	0.009
T-statistic	1.61	−0.183

Sources: Ys: © *Stocks, Bonds, Bills, and Inflation 1996 Yearbook™,* Ibbotson Associates, Chicago (annually updates work by Roger G. Ibbotson and Rex. A. Sinquefield). Used with permission. All rights reserved. Xs: Standard & Poor's. Used with permission of Standard & Poor's, a division of the McGraw-Hill Companies.

TABLE 2-3

Pairwise Correlations between Potential Predictor Variables for Stock Market Returns (1942–1992)*

	Correlation
Dividend yield versus PE ratio	–0.85
Dividend yield versus earnings yield	0.87
PE ratio versus earnings yield	–0.95

*Note the correlation between the PE ratio and the earnings yield. Given one, we know the other with certainty—PE is the reciprocal of earnings yield (EP)—but the relationship between a number X and its reciprocal $1/X$ is not linear. Hence, we have the less-than-perfect negative correlation between the two.

Source: Standard & Poor's. Used with permission of Standard & Poor's, a division of the McGraw-Hill Companies.

dividend yield alone, the R-squared is 0.19, meaning that the dividend yield explains 19 percent of the squared variation in stock returns. The R-squared for the dividend yield/PE model is also 0.19. Moreover, the t-statistics dropped sharply for both dividend yield and PE in the two–predictor variable model. What's going on here?

The problem is that dividend yield and PE, to a large degree, carry the same information. Since very little new information comes with the addition of PE, the R-squared for the two–predictor variable model doesn't budge relative to the R-squared for the dividend yield model. Correlations shown in Table 2–3 confirm this. The correlation between dividend yield and PE is –0.85, indicating that the two are highly negatively correlated.

Now let's consider the issue of the t-statistics. Why did they go down so sharply? Recall that the t-statistic is the ratio between the X-coefficient and its standard error. A large t-statistic means that the standard error is small relative to the X-coefficient. When this occurs, we are confident about the estimate of the X-coefficient.

Now let's step back and review the interpretation of the X-coefficients for a two–predictor variable model. The first

X-coefficient tells us how the forecast varies as we vary the first X-variable, assuming that the second X-variable is held constant. The second X-coefficient is similarly interpreted. Here's the problem: the dividend yield (the first X-variable) and PE ratio (the second X-variable) are highly negatively correlated. That means when one moves up, the other moves down. So it is virtually impossible to vary the first X-variable while holding the other X-variable constant. The sharp drop in the t-statistics, indicating a sharp drop in the confidence in the estimates of the X-coefficients, hints that the high correlation between the two X-variables, what statisticians call **collinearity,** is a problem in the regression model with dividend yield and the PE ratio.

Could we have predicted this problem in advance? Perhaps. Note the following:

$$\text{Dividend Yield} = \text{Dividends}/\text{Price}$$
$$\text{PE} = 1/(\text{Earnings}/\text{Price})$$

Since the dividends paid are highly correlated to earnings (companies tend to pay a stable percentage of earnings as dividends), we might have suspected that dividend yields and PE ratios are highly (negatively) correlated—that as dividend yields rise, PE ratios fall and vice versa.

Continued discussion of collinearity will follow. Suffice it to say for now, however, that one of the tricks of regression analysis is to find predictor variables with nonoverlapping information. That is, for starters, predictor variables should be correlated with the forecast variable. But correlations between pairs of predictor variables should not be excessively high.

MECHANIZING THE SEARCH PROCESS

We still have several predictor variable candidates that could improve the dividend yield regression model. We could try adding the other variables one at a time to see if the R-squared rises significantly. After finding the variable that adds the most to the *R*-squared, we could try to find the "best" third variable to add to the model in the same manner. As long as the *t*-statistics for each predictor variable remain greater than 2 or less than –2, we can be reasonably confident that each predictor variable belongs in the model.

One way to mechanize testing combinations of potential predictor variables is to use a procedure called **stepwise regression.** In forward stepwise regression, a statistical software program finds the best first variable for the model, then the next best variable and so on. In backwards stepwise regression, the user can start with a model that includes all of the potential predictor variables (also known as the *kitchen sink model*). The stepwise program software then eliminates variables systematically. In both the forward and backward processes, variables added or eliminated must meet criteria chosen by the user.

Using stepwise regression is controversial, however, so much so that some statistical software package makers refuse to include the process in their programs. Analysts who scorn the process are concerned that stepwise regression will create a model that looks good but may be the result of chance. If, for example, an analyst is trying to predict stock market returns, he or she could easily find hundreds of economic and market-related variables to test. But given 100 potential candidates, it would be unusual not to find a few variables that are statistically significant as a result of chance alone. Many analysts would prefer to have a good reason to believe that a potential predictor variable was a good one before testing the variable.

The purer alternative, then, is to pick variables that theoretically are likely to be good predictors. On the other hand, when a large class of variables is thought to contain forecast potential, a promising variable could be discovered and perhaps justified theoretically after the discovery. For example, we might believe that the level of, or changes in, short-term interest rates should help in forecasting stock prices. But we know there are many ways to measure short-term interest rates, including yields on Treasury bills, commercial paper, federal funds, bankers' acceptances, and certificates of deposit as well as the prime rate, the discount rate, and Eurodollar deposit rates. If it were true that theory dictated that a certain rate should work better than the others, should the others be discarded and not tested? Definitely not, if only because theory is often imperfect at explaining the real world.

The purer alternative may be preferred by many, but to discard a potentially good predictor because it was not specifically postulated ahead of time could limit the ultimate effectiveness of a model. In the end, variables selected for a model should be meaningful or there is no reason to believe they will continue to work in the future. Exactly when justification for including a variable is sufficient is a subjective issue. In practice, good analysts probably can justify on some rational grounds most of the variables they use in building their models. But in the give and take of the research process there are surprises that often make a lot of sense after they are discovered. It would be a waste not to take advantage of them.[7]

A STOCK MARKET MODEL
USING THREE PREDICTOR VARIABLES

Will we ever improve our dividend yield model? Table 2–4 shows the regression output for a model that includes three of the variables listed in Table 2–1, the dividend yield, the change in the spread between Baa and Aaa corporate bond yields, and the gross domestic product deflator.

First let's consider why the spread and deflator variables might belong in a model designed to forecast the stock market. The Aaa yield is the yield on corporate bonds rated Aaa, the highest credit rating issued by Moody's, a well-regarded rating agency. Bonds rated Baa are of significantly lower quality. If the spread or difference between Baa and Aaa yields is narrow, then bond investors are comfortable owning lower quality bonds,

TABLE 2-4

Regression Output for the Stock Market versus the Dividend Yield, Credit Spread, and GDP Deflator*

	Constant	−0.10		
	Standard error of Y estimate	0.14		
	R-squared	0.31		
	Number of observations	51		
		Dividend Yield	**Spread**	**Deflator**
		X_1	X_2	X_3
X-coefficient		7.07	0.19	−0.014
Standard error of X-coefficient		1.73	0.08	0.007
T-statistic		4.09	2.42	−2.01

*The estimation period is 1942–1992.

Sources: Y: © *Stocks, Bonds, Bills, and Inflation 1996 Yearbook™*, Ibbotson Associates, Chicago (annually updates work by Roger G. Ibbotson and Rex A. Sinquefield). Used with permission. All rights reserved.
X1: Standard & Poor's. Used with permission of Standard & Poor's, a division of the McGraw-Hill Companies.
X2: Moody's Investor Services. Used with permission.
X3: U.S. Department of Commerce.

probably reflecting their forecast of a good economy in the months ahead and little likelihood that the companies that issued the bonds are going to have problems meeting their debt obligations. A wide credit spread means just the opposite, that holding lower quality bonds is risky. In short, a narrow spread probably implies a forecast of a good economy and a wide spread, a poor economy.

The surprise, of course, is that the change in the spread is positively correlated with future stock price changes. That is, a widening spread (meaning less confidence in the economy) is generally followed by rising stock prices. This counterintuitive result may reflect the cyclical nature of the economy. Recessions are followed by expansions. So when the credit spread is widening, perhaps indicating a poor economy, forward-looking investors may buy stocks in anticipation of better times ahead.

The gross domestic product deflator is an estimate of inflation for all goods and services produced in the United States. Although stock returns have exceeded general inflation measures over time and thus are thought of as a good hedge against inflation, the fact is, stocks often perform poorly when price inflation is rising. Since rising inflation typically leads to higher interest rates and theory does dictate that stocks are worth less in a high-interest-rate environment than they are in a low-interest-rate environment, then inflation should be negatively correlated with stock prices.

Now let's consider the regression output in Table 2–4. Notice that the R-squared rose from 0.19 for the model with dividend yield alone, to 0.31 for the model with the three predictor variables. All of the t-statistics are greater than +2 or less than −2, indicating that each variable probably belongs in the model. The signs are in line with expectations as well. Dividend yield has a positive sign, as it did in our original model. The deflator variable has a negative sign, indicating that rising inflation generally reduces the probability that stock prices will rise. Finally, the change in the credit spread maintains its counterintuitive positive sign.

Recall now that the deflator variable alone (as shown in Table 2–1) has a negligible correlation (0.02) with stock returns. Somehow, however, the deflator became a significant predictor in combination with the dividend yield and credit spread variables. Should we be suspicious of this outcome?

The answer is probably not. In order to explain the sudden significance of the deflator variable, we need to look at the so-called **residuals** of the regression model. The residuals are calculated by subtracting the actual value of the forecast variable from the regression forecast. Perhaps the easiest way to visualize residuals is to turn back to Figure 1–2 on page 10. Points on the regression line show model forecasts of stock market returns (measured on the vertical axis) for all levels of the dividend yield (measured on the horizontal axis). The individual points represent actual stock market returns for each year and the actual dividend yield at the end of the previous year. The residuals are represented by the vertical distance between the points and the regression line (shown as the distance d for one of the points). When a point representing an actual value is above the regression line, the residual is positive; points below the regression line have negative residuals. An example showing the mechanics of a regression and how the residuals are calculated is shown in Appendix 1.

How did the deflator variable become significant in combination with the dividend yield and credit spread variables? The regression model with dividend yield and credit spread as predictor variables explains about 25 percent of the squared variation of stock market returns. The 75 percent of the squared variation left unexplained is represented by the residuals. So, while the deflator variable has virtually no correlation with stock market returns, it does have a significant correlation (–0.26) with the residuals of the regression model with dividend yield and credit spread. In other words, the deflator variable has a –0.26 correlation with the squared variation left unexplained by the regression model with dividend yield and credit spread. So the addition of the deflator variable lifts the R-squared, in this case, from 0.25 to 0.31.

This outcome offers further insight into how we might look for explanatory variables. Initially, variables that have high correlations with the forecast variable might be explored. But as the model develops it might become more useful to focus on variables that correlate well with the unexplained squared variation of the forecast variable, the residuals, rather than continuing to focus on explanatory variables that correlate well with the forecast variable itself.

The variables listed in Table 2–1 appear in Appendix 2. Explore the data, duplicate the results reported in this chapter, and create an altogether new model for forecasting stock market returns. One change that seems to improve the model shown in Table 2–3 is to put the reciprocal of dividend yield (1/(Dividend Yield)), in place of the dividend yield variable. Does this change make sense?

3

ADDITIONAL TOPICS ON REGRESSION MODELS WITH SEVERAL PREDICTOR VARIABLES

HOW MANY VARIABLES?

Regression analysis allows us to forecast a variable, such as stock market returns, using one or more predictor variables. A question that arises is: How many predictor variables should a model have? Unfortunately, there is no answer based on a formula. One potential approach is to consider whether a proposed model has too many predictor variables by asking the following questions about each predictor variable:

1. Does inclusion of the variable make sense?
2. Is there a reason to believe that the variable will continue to act with respect to the forecast variable as it has in the past?
3. Would omission of the variable reduce the explanatory power of the model significantly?

If the answer to each of the above three questions is yes, then the variable probably belongs in the model.

If we assume that all predictor variables pass questions 1 and 2, then all we must consider is the marginal contribution of each variable. Suppose, for example, that a regression model with five predictor variables has an R-squared of 0.59. If the removal of one predictor variable reduces the R-squared to 0.57, then that predictor variable might reasonably be omitted.

One reason to be suspicious of variables that lift the R-squared measure only modestly is to consider that the R-squared measure is guaranteed to rise as new predictor variables are added to a model. This property is demonstrated rather dramatically in Table 3–1. A spreadsheet program was used to generate 12 random observations of a hypothetical forecast variable. Eleven hypothetical predictor variables, each with 12 observations, also were created using the spreadsheet's random number generator. So we have 12 randomly generated observations each of a forecast variable and 11 predictor variables. Table 3–1 shows the regression output for 10 regressions. In the first, the forecast or Y variable was regressed against the first predictor variable (X_1). In the second regression, the Y variable was regressed against the first and second predictor variables $(X_1$ and $X_2)$. This process was continued until a 10th run in which the Y variable was regressed against the first 10 predictor variables $(X_1, X_2, ..., X_{10})$.

The R-squared for the first regression is 0.03. With each successive regression, the R-squared advances, eventually to a hefty 0.96 in the 10th regression. (Some statistical packages would have allowed a run of an 11th regression, showing a perfect R-squared of 1, but the program used for this example flashed an error message on the 11th run.) Of course, the R-squared is nonsense. Indeed, if we were to add some observations to the data set and use the last regression run to create forecasts, we would find that model had no explanatory power.

Since adding nonsense predictor variables increases the R-squared statistic, researchers have to be on guard that an increased R-squared due to the addition of a predictor variable

TABLE 3-1

Regression Output for a 12-Observation Problem

Constant	0.58
Standard error of Y estimate	0.30
R-squared	0.03
Number of observations	12

	Random X_1
X-coefficient	−0.18
Standard error of X-coefficient	0.30
T-statistic	−0.60

Constant	0.41
Standard error of Y estimate	0.28
R-Squared	0.22
Number of observations	12

	Random X_1	Random X_2
X-coefficient	−0.17	0.37
Standard error of X-coefficient	0.28	0.26
T-statistic	−0.62	1.46

Constant	0.12
Standard error of Y estimate	0.21
R-squared	0.60
Number of observations	12

	Random X_1	Random X_2	Random X_3
X-coefficient	−0.61	0.79	0.91
Standard error of X-coefficient	0.27	0.25	0.34
T-statistic	−2.28	3.19	2.73

TABLE 3-1

Regression Output for a 12-Observation Problem *(continued)*

Constant	0.10				
Standard error of Y estimate	0.23				
R-squared	0.60				
Number of observations	12				
	Random X_1	Random X_2	Random X_3	Random X_4	
X-coefficient	−0.62	0.80	0.91	0.03	
Standard error of X-coefficient	0.29	0.27	0.36	0.23	
T-statistic	−2.13	2.94	2.56	0.14	
Constant	−0.01				
Standard error of Y estimate	0.24				
R-squared	0.61				
Number of observations	12				
	Random X_1	Random X_2	Random X_3	Random X_4	Random X_5
X-coefficient	−0.62	0.85	0.90	0.01	0.18
Standard error of X-coefficient	0.31	0.30	0.38	0.25	0.35
T-statistic	−2.01	2.80	2.39	0.03	0.51
Constant	−0.25				
Standard error of Y estimate	0.26				
R-squared	0.64				
Number of observations	12				
	Random X_1	Random X_2	Random X_3	Random X_4	Random X_5	Random X_6
X-coefficient	−0.57	0.83	0.87	0.10	0.30	0.26
Standard error of X-coefficient	0.34	0.32	0.41	0.32	0.43	0.45
T-statistic	−1.68	2.58	2.15	0.32	0.70	0.57

TABLE 3-1

Regression Output for a 12-Observation Problem (*continued*)

Constant	-0.33
Standard error of Y estimate	0.23
R-squared	0.76
Number of observations	12

	Random X_1	Random X_2	Random X_3	Random X_4	Random X_5	Random X_6	Random X_7
X-coefficient	-0.65	1.08	1.05	0.28	-0.17	-0.08	0.56
Standard error of X-coefficient	0.31	0.34	0.39	0.32	0.51	0.47	0.39
T-statistic	-2.06	3.16	2.69	0.90	-0.32	-0.17	1.42

Constant	0.57
Standard error of Y estimate	0.21
R-squared	0.86
Number of observations	12

	Random X_1	Random X_2	Random X_3	Random X_4	Random X_5	Random X_6	Random X_7	Random X_8
X-coefficient	-0.83	1.33	1.28	-0.09	-0.53	-0.83	0.51	-0.50
Standard error of X-coefficient	0.31	0.35	0.38	0.39	0.52	0.67	0.35	0.35
T-statistic	-2.70	3.78	3.34	-0.24	-1.01	-1.23	1.46	-1.43

Constant	0.40
Standard error of Y estimate	0.25
R-squared	0.86
Number of observations	12

TABLE 3-1

Regression Output for a 12-Observation Problem (concluded)

	Random X_1	Random X_2	Random X_3	Random X_4	Random X_5	Random X_6	Random X_7	Random X_8
X-coefficient	-0.76	1.24	1.20	-0.04	-0.45	-0.68	0.45	-0.43
Standard error of X-coefficient	0.44	0.54	0.54	0.50	0.68	0.97	0.48	0.50
T-statistic	-1.74	2.32	2.25	-0.09	-0.66	-0.70	0.95	-0.86

	Random X_9
	0.11
	0.40
	0.27

Constant	-0.18
Standard error of Y estimate	0.19
R-squared	0.96
Number of observations	12

	Random X_1	Random X_2	Random X_3	Random X_4	Random X_5	Random X_6	Random X_7	Random X_8
X-coefficient	-0.54	1.41	1.35	-0.32	-0.27	-0.62	0.13	-0.72
Standard error of X-coefficient	0.36	0.42	0.42	0.42	0.53	0.74	0.41	0.42
T-statistic	-1.49	3.36	3.26	-0.77	-0.50	-0.85	0.32	-1.70

	Random X_9	Random X_{10}
	0.44	0.75
	0.37	0.48
	1.19	1.58

A randomly generated Y is regressed against a randomly generated X_1, then X_1 and X_2, then X_1, X_2 and X_3, and so on. Notice how the R-squared for the regression increases as the number of predictor variables increases.

may be the result of chance. One way to control for the tendency of the R-squared to drift upward as predictor variables are added is to look at a second measure of R-squared called the **adjusted R-squared** or **corrected R-squared,** which is calculated by virtually all regression software packages. The adjusted R-squared is also called R-bar squared, because the R is often written with a macron (horizontal bar) over it in statistics books and programs.

Without going into how the adjusted R-squared is calculated, note that its value takes into consideration the number of variables in a regression model. Adding new variables will always increase the R-squared, but the adjusted R-squared could rise or fall. Another important property of the adjusted R-squared is that its value can fall below zero. Since it is impossible to explain a negative percentage of a forecast variable's squared variation, a negative adjusted R-squared is assumed to be zero. In sum, when the same forecast variable is used in competing models with different numbers of predictor variables, the adjusted R-squared typically gives a better indication as to which model is better than the R-squared measure.

MORE ON CORRELATION

In Chapter 2 we discussed the possibility of quickly testing a group of predictor variable candidates against a forecast variable by running a correlation analysis. Most statistical software packages will create what is called a correlation matrix for any list of variables in one command. The correlation matrix lists the correlation for each pair of variables. Typically, if the matrix shows the correlation between two variables, X_1 and X_2, then it will not show the correlation between X_2 and X_1, because the two correlations are equal.

When a correlation is very close to zero, it is safe to say that there is no linear relationship between the two variables under consideration. If the correlation is large, say 0.70 or –0.70, then there is a strong linear relationship between the variables. But what if a correlation amounts to 0.12 or –0.12? How can we determine if there is a statistically significant relationship between the variables?

One way is to run a regression between the forecast variable and predictor variable and look at the *t*-statistic, from which we can determine the probability that the regression coefficient does not equal zero. If there are at least 60 observations in the regression, a *t*-statistic of 2 or –2 means there is about a 95 percent probability that the regression coefficient does not equal 0. A *t*-statistic of 2.39 or –2.39 for the same sample would indicate about a 98 percent probability; a value of 2.66 or –2.66 would indicate a 99 percent probability. Since a 95 percent probability is often considered to be sufficient evidence of a statistically significant relationship, many people use the following rule of thumb: if the *t*-statistic is less than –2 or greater than 2, then the correlation is considered to be significant, or not likely to be due to chance. Most statistics books have tables that can be used to find the probability that a relationship is due to chance, based on the number of observations and the *t*-statistic. Most statistical software packages also print the probability that a regression coefficient equals zero.

INFLUENCE POINTS

Once a predictor variable moves from candidate status to more serious consideration, it is a good idea to plot the forecast variable against the predictor variable, in other words, to create a scatter plot in which the forecast variable appears on the Y or vertical axis and the predictor variable is on the X or horizontal axis. Plotting the relationship is important because a single point can act like a lever and account for virtually all of the correlation. How this happens is probably best shown through an example.

In this example the forecast variable is the total return on the S&P 500 for each month from January 1984 through December

1992. The predictor or X-variable was constructed from open interest data on exchange traded index put and call options.

Many stock market watchers monitor put and call option data for their ability to forecast short-term swings in the market. The owner of an American-style call option has the right but not the obligation to buy an asset for a specified price on or before a specified date. An American-style put option offers the right but not the obligation to sell an asset for a specified price on or before a specified date. In practice, the holder of a call (put) option has made a leveraged bet that the underlying asset is going to rise (fall).

Put and call buying, in the aggregate, is thought to be a contrary indicator because when investors are buying more calls (i.e., when they are bullish), the stock market tends to be weak. Likewise, when option buyers are bearish (i.e., when put buying prevails over call buying), the market tends to be firm.

In order to construct the predictor variable for our sample data set, the number of open put positions (or open interest) on the OEX 100 was divided by the number of open call positions each day. (Note that many practitioners prefer to look at ratios of put and call volume rather than put and call open interest.) A figure for each month was calculated by averaging the daily observations. Finally, the change in the monthly ratio was calculated by subtracting the previous month's ratio from the current month's ratio.

In this case, the predictor variable has a 0.155 correlation with the forecast variable. But a quick look at Figure 3–1 shows that a single point in the bottom left-hand corner is acting like a lever. Without that point, the correlation falls to an insignificant 0.016. The fact that virtually all the correlation is due to one point more or less disqualifies the predictor variable from more serious consideration. (For the curious, the observation in question was for October 1987, the month the stock market crashed.)

There are other ways to find leverage, also called **influence points.** First, some statistical software packages have routines

FIGURE 3-1

An Example of an Influence Point

Notice the influence point in the bottom left-hand corner. The correlation between the forecast variable and the predictor variable is 0.155. When the influence point is excluded, the correlation drops to an insignificant 0.016.

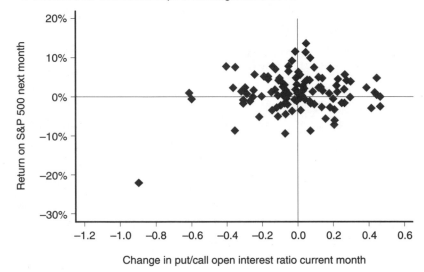

Change in put/call open interest ratio current month

that identify influence points. Second, observations can be eliminated, one at a time, when running a correlation or regression analysis. If the correlation or R-squared measure drops sharply on the removal of any single observation, then that observation may well be an influence point. A third way to find leverage when reviewing a multivariable regression analysis is to consider the following procedure.

Suppose the regression has three predictor variables, X_1, X_2, and X_3. First, run a regression using only X_1 and X_2 and calculate the residuals. (Recall that the residual, or error term, is the difference between the actual and fitted forecast variable. If these terms are confusing, a review of the mechanics of a regression appears in Appendix 1.) Then plot X_3 against those residuals, and study the plot for the existence of influence points. Alternatively, run a series of correlation analyses between X_3 and the residuals, removing one observation at a time. If the correlation falls sharply upon the removal of a single point, then X_3 is suspect as a forecast variable in the regression under consideration. Repeat this process to determine if X_1 or X_2 have any influence points relative to the other predictor variables in the regression model.

MORE ON COLLINEARITY

In Chapter 2 we saw how the inclusion of two highly correlated predictor variables can make regression output hard to interpret. We concluded that correlations between predictor variables should not be excessively high. The existence of high correlation between two predictor variables in a regression model creates a condition called collinearity. Now suppose that we have more than two predictor variables in a regression model. If every pairwise correlation between the predictor variables is checked, can we be sure that correlation among them is not a problem?

The answer is no, because it is possible that one of the predictor variables could be "correlated" with a combination of the other predictor variables, creating a condition called **multicollinearity.** (Note that in a regression with one predictor variable, the square of the correlation R between the forecast and predictor variables is the R-squared for the regression. When a regression has more than one predictor variable, the positive square root of the R-squared is called the multiple R. Hence, the term **multicollinearity.**) One way to check for multicollinearity is to run one regression for each predictor variable. If, for example, a regression had five predictor variables (X_1, X_2, X_3, X_4, X_5), then five regressions would be run: first X_1 against X_2, X_3, X_4, and X_5; then X_2 against X_1, X_3, X_4, and X_5 and so on. If the R-squared for any of the regressions turns out to be excessively high, then multicollinearity could be a problem with the model.

To conclude, checking for multicollinearity is a rather straightforward process. In order to avoid it, we can remove predictor variables that are excessively correlated with any combination of the other predictor variables.

Now the question is: How do we decide when a predictor variable is too highly correlated with the other predictor variables? The following rule of thumb can be helpful: If the multiple correlations between each predictor variable and the remaining predictor variables all fall below 0.85 (R-squared = 0.72), then multicollinearity probably is not a tremendous problem; if any of the multiple correlations exceed 0.85, then multicollinearity may well be problematic and the predictor variable(s) involved might be removed or reconfigured. The choice of 0.85 is somewhat arbitrary. As the multiple R for this test approaches 0.85, uncertainty regarding the regression coefficients increases gradually, but when the multiple R rises above 0.85, the uncertainty takes off in an exponential fashion.[8]

One last (and important) note on multicollinearity: When the condition exists, it is the predictor coefficients for which we have little confidence, not the model forecasts. So in theory, since we are more concerned about forecasts than regression output, multicollinearity should not bother us except in extreme cases. But when one predictor variable is highly correlated with the rest of the predictor variables, then little new information is being introduced to the model by that predictor variable. Checking for multicollinearity can thus be considered a way of determining why the addition of a predictor variable does not add to the R-squared of a model. If the addition of a predictor variable does not increase the R-squared, a high multiple R between the new predictor variable and the rest of the predictor variables means that most of the information the new variable has to offer has already been captured by the original predictor variables.

MORE ABOUT CONFIGURING FORECAST AND PREDICTOR VARIABLES

When reviewing candidates for predictor variables in Chapter 2, we noted three basic ways to configure a variable: as a level, a change in level, and a "change in change" of a level. The S&P 500, the Consumer Price Index, and the yield on 30-year Treasury bonds are all examples of variables expressed as levels. If we refer to the Consumer Price Index in symbols as *CPI* then there are two simple ways to express a change in the variable. One way is to calculate the percent change (in this case over six months):

$$(CPI_0 / CPI_{-6}) - 1$$

where CPI_0 is the CPI level in the current month, and CPI_{-6} is the CPI level six months previous to the current month.

A second way to calculate a change is to use subtraction:

$$CPI_0 - CPI_{-6}$$

In the case of the Consumer Price Index, the percent change is the preferred specification of change. That's because the CPI trends upward over time. In the 1960s the index (set to 100 in the 1982–84 period) registered levels on the order of 30. In the mid-1990s, the levels were approximately 150. If subtraction is used, then a move in the 1960s from 30 to 33 is seen as equivalent in a model as a move in the 1990s from 150 to 153. Using the simple difference, both changes are three index points. Clearly, the magnitude of the three-point change in the 1960s should be seen as larger than an equal point move in the 1990s. The percent change calculation makes the distinction between the equal point differences by appropriately adjusting for the two base values.

When a variable fluctuates more or less evenly about some middle value, then the simple difference will work well in a model as a measure of change. Such nontrending variables are said to be stationary. Changes in interest rates, for example, can be measured using subtraction. Indeed, a rise in rates from 5 percent to 6 percent is typically referred to as a one-percentage-point increase (6 minus 5), rather than a 20 percent increase (1 divided by 5) in rates.

Nevertheless, some analysts will argue against using differences to measure changes in interest rates. The argument against using subtraction might start with the question: Will a change in rates from 5 percent to 6 percent have the same affect on a variable of interest as a rise from 10 percent to 11 percent? Someone who believes that the equal percentage point moves are not equivalent might favor percent changes in interest rates over simple differences.

A third way to measure the change in a variable, similar to the percent change calculation, is to use the natural logarithm function. Easily calculated by spreadsheet and statistical software, the natural logarithm can be thought of as a sort of compromise between two different percent change calculations. If a variable moves from 100 to 120, the conventional way of calculating the percent change is to divide 20 by 100 to get 20 percent. But if 120 rather than 100 is used as the denominator, then the answer becomes 20/120, or 16.7 percent. The natural logarithm of the change, written as $ln(120/100)$, is 0.182, which is between 16.7 percent and 20 percent.

Some analysts prefer the natural log as a way of expressing percent changes, especially when some of the percent changes under consideration are very large. Table 3–2 shows how percent changes compare to natural logarithms.

The logarithm function also can be put to good use when charting a trending variable like the Consumer Price Index. As we discussed earlier, a 10 percent move on a base of 30 (in the 1960s) is three index points. In the mid-1990s the same percentage move (on a base of about 150) is 15 index points. This means that similar percentage changes look bigger as time progresses owing to the steadily rising base. As a result, the slope of the curve gets steeper and steeper as time progresses, though not

TABLE 3–2

The Natural Logarithm as a Measure of Percent Change*

Percent Change	Holding Period Return	Natural Logarithm
–60%	0.40	–0.92
–50	0.50	–0.69
–40	0.60	–0.51
–30	0.70	–0.36
–20	0.80	–0.22
–10	0.90	–0.11
0	1.00	0.00
10	1.10	0.10
20	1.20	0.18
30	1.30	0.26
40	1.40	0.34
50	1.50	0.41
60	1.60	0.47
70	1.70	0.53
80	1.80	0.59
90	1.90	0.64
100	2.00	0.69

*The table shows that the natural log reduces positive percent changes and increases the absolute value of negative percent changes. The difference between the natural log and percent change widens as the absolute value of the change increases.

necessarily because of ever-increasing rates of inflation. The logarithm will adjust for the creeping base phenomenon so that equal percentage changes will cover the same vertical distance on a chart, regardless of the level of the index. As a result, the logarithm of an index growing at a constant rate will plot as a straight line, in contrast to an ever-steepening curve when the index is plotted arithmetically, as shown in Figure 3–2.

The third major way of configuring a variable, the "change in the change" of a level, can normally be calculated as the difference between two changes, since changes in variables tend to be stationary. Price acceleration, for example, might be defined as

F I G U R E   3–2

The Effect of the Logarithm Function on a Variable with a Constrant Growth Trend

The first chart shows an index growing at a 7.5 percent annual rate. The arithmetic plot gives the impression that the index is growing at an ever-increasing rate. The second plot shows the natural log of the index. Notice the constant growth rate is represented as a line.

Index Growing at a 7.5% Annual Rate

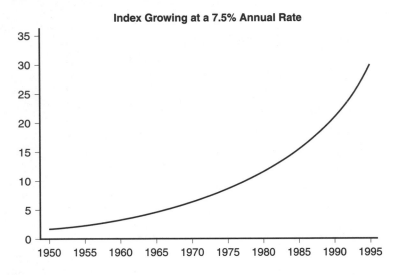

Natural Log of the Index

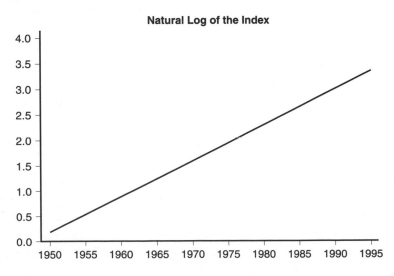

$$(CPI_0 / CPI_{-6}) - (CPI_{-6} / CPI_{-12})$$

where CPI_0 is the Consumer Price Index in the current month and CPI_{-6} and CPI_{-12} are the Consumer Price Index 6 and 12 months prior to the current month, respectively. Although we usually subtract one from the ratio in order create a percentage, in this case the ones cancel out. The first term measures the percent change in the most recent six-month period; the second term, the same change in the previous six-month period. Price acceleration is the difference between the two percent changes.

The three basic forms, level, change, and change in change, are shown for the Consumer Price Index in Figure 3–3. Notice how the plot of the level trends upward and gradually steepens. The percent change fluctuates more or less smoothly about a central tendency, although it is fair to say that the inflationary trend of the 1970s can still be seen. The change in the percent change (calculated by subtracting the previous value of percent change from the current value) is completely devoid of a trend. The amplitude of the oscillations on the acceleration chart does tell us that there was a short burst of inflation in the early 1950s, followed by 20 years of relative stability. In 1975, the fluctuations widen again, indicating the presence of larger swings in inflation.

The issue of whether to configure a variable as a level, change, or change in change is especially important when choosing the forecast variable for a model. In general, using a level as the forecast variable is not a good idea. For example, if the monthly level of the S&P 500 is used as the forecast variable for a stock market model, using the previous month's level as a predictor variable will yield an R-squared on the order of 0.99+, as shown in Table 3–3.

The near-perfect R-squared is an illusion. To see why this is true, suppose the current month's level is 500. If a typical monthly percent change is between –5 percent and +5 percent, then the next month's level is likely to fall between 475 and 525.

F I G U R E   3–3

Three Forms of Configuring the Consumer Price Index

The first is the level of the CPI, which clearly trends upward. The second is the six-month percent change, which removes the bulk of the trend component. The third shows the "change in the change" of the CPI, in this case, the six-month difference between percent change figures.

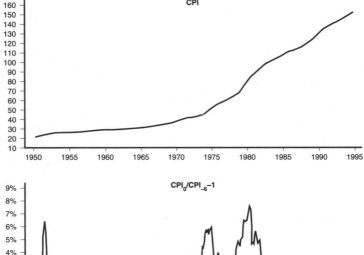

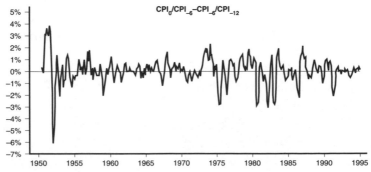

Source: U.S. Department of Labor.

TABLE 3-3

Regression Output for a Model*

Constant	−0.189
Standard error of Y estimate	6.322
R-squared	0.997
Number of observations	360
X-coefficient	1.008
Standard error of X-coefficient	0.003
T-statistic	329.472

*In this model the monthly level of the S&P 500 is the forecast variable and the previous month's value is the predictor variable. The near-perfect R-squared is an illusion—in reality this model has virtually no explanatory power. The X-coefficient greater than one indicates that stocks have risen, on average, over the estimation period from 1964–93.

Source: Standard & Poor's. Used with permission of Standard & Poor's, a division of the McGraw-Hill Companies.

The typical potential error against an estimate of 500 is between −25 and +25. The size of the potential error is small compared to the magnitude of the variable; hence, the exceedingly high R-squared in the regression output. Actually, the model will forecast a level slightly higher than the previous month's level, reflecting the tendency for stocks to rise over time. But there is virtually no information in the forecasts. The preferred alternative is to choose a forecast variable in a change format like percent change or the logarithm function. The reported R-squared will be sharply lower, but it will be an honest measure of the model's explanatory power.

MORE ON SQUARED VARIATION

In Chapter 1 we defined R-squared in terms of total squared variation of a forecast variable from its mean. Let's run through a sample calculation for a variable Y that has five observations.

Y	Y_{avg}	$Y - Y_{avg}$	$(Y - Y_{avg})^2$
2	5	−3	9
7	5	2	4
4	5	−1	1
3	5	−2	4
9	5	4	16
Total Squared Variation			34

Sometimes analysts find it useful to work with the average rather than total squared variation. In the example above, the average squared variation is the total squared variation divided by the number of observations, or $34/5 = 6.8$. The average squared variation is called the **variance.**

A companion to the concept of variance is the **standard deviation,** which is the positive square root of the variance. Both the standard deviation and variance are used as measures of dispersion or volatility. From an investment point of view, the standard deviation and variance of a series of monthly stock market returns is considered an estimate of the risk of owning equities. The higher the value for these measures of volatility, the higher the risk.

The standard deviation has some very useful properties. If a group of observations like stock market returns is normally distributed, about 68 percent of the observations will fall between plus or minus one standard deviation from the average of the stock market returns. What does this mean? Suppose we have a column of 100 stock market returns in a spreadsheet and, using the method in the example above, we calculate that the total squared variation is 14,400. The variance would be $14,400/100 = 144$ and the standard deviation would be the positive square root of 144, or 12. Now suppose the average of the 100 returns is 10. Assuming the return distribution is normal, we can estimate that 68 out of 100 of the returns (68 percent) will fall between the mean, plus or minus one standard deviation. In the current example:

FIGURE 3–4

The Normal Distribution

The percentages of the area under the curve bounded by integer multiples of the standard deviation from the mean are shown. The normal distribution assumption for asset returns will allow forecasts to be transformed into probabilities in Section 3.

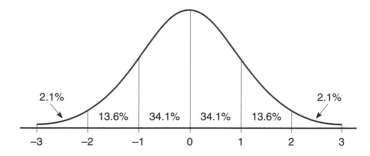

$$\text{Mean} - 1\ sd = 10 - 12 = -2$$
$$\text{Mean} + 1\ sd = 10 + 12 = 22$$

so that we would expect about 68 out of the 100 observations to fall between –2 percent and +22 percent.

Now, if the range is widened to include plus or minus two standard deviations from the mean, then

$$\text{Mean} - 2\ sd = 10 - 24 = -14$$
$$\text{Mean} + 2\ sd = 10 + 24 = \ 34$$

and approximately 95 percent of the stock returns will fall between –14 percent and +34 percent. If the net is cast out even further to include plus or minus three standard deviations, then virtually all of the returns (an expected percentage of 99.7 percent) will be included. A plot of the normal distribution is shown in Figure 3–4.

While it is true that stock and bond market returns are not perfectly normal, they are close enough to put the assumption to good work. Later we will use the normality assumption in

Section III to transform forecasts into statements like "there is a 64 percent probability that asset X will outperform asset Y."

Here's how the idea works. Suppose that stock returns are normally distributed with a mean of 10 percent annually and a standard deviation of 20 percent, in line with the historical record over the last 70 years. What are the odds that next year's return will be positive? Referring to Figure 3–5, we note there is a 50 percent probability that next year's return will be 10 percent or more. That's because 10 percent is in the middle of the possible outcomes and the distribution of possible outcomes is symmetric about the mean. Now, the space between 0 percent and 10 percent is 10 percentage points, or one-half of the 20 percent standard deviation. According to normal distribution tables, an outcome within that range represents 19.1 percent of the possible outcomes. Hence, the probability of a return greater than 0 percent equals 69.1 percent (19.1 percent + 50 percent).

The example above allows us to define *forecast* somewhat precisely. A forecast is an estimate of the mean of a distribution of possible returns some time into the future. Thus, if we forecast a 10 percent return in the next year and the actual outcome is 15 percent, the forecast may not have been wrong because there is no way to know the real distribution of possible returns. Indeed, the forecast may have been right, and the actual outcome just turned out to be a little bit greater than the mean of the distribution of possible returns.

FIGURE 3–5

The Normal Distribution

In this case the mean return forecast is 10 percent and the standard deviation is 20 percent. Since the normal distribution is symmetric about its mean, returns greater than 10 percent represent 50 percent of the possible outcomes. The space between 0 percent and 10 percent is one-half of a standard deviation. According to normal distribution tables, the range of returns between 0 percent and 10 percent represent 19.1 percent of the possible outcomes. The probability of a return greater than 0 percent then, is 69.1 percent, if the assumption about the distribution are correct.

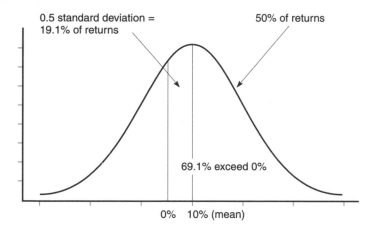

SECTION

II

FOUR MARKET TIMING MODELS

CHAPTER

4

A STOCK
MARKET MODEL

As a portfolio manager in the mid-1980s, I had the privilege (or chore) of reviewing a two-foot pile of Wall Street research each day. The reports often included the work of strategists who claimed that certain indicators were useful in forecasting the stock or bond market. Some of the work was unconvincing. A standard style of presentation, still in use today, showed the stock market plotted above an oscillating indicator. Up and down arrows throughout the chart marked buy and sell signals in a way that was supposed to validate the indicator's explanatory power.

Based on a visual examination of the data alone, however, it was difficult to gauge an indicator's value. The charts often covered 30 years of data, making it virtually impossible to really know if an indicator on average led, was coincident with, or lagged the market it was supposed to forecast. (For purposes of forecasting, only an indicator that leads a market is useful.) Still another concern with this type of presentation was that the buy and sell signals were chosen with the benefit of 20–20 hindsight, raising the concern that future performance of the indicator would not match apparent past performance.

The growing availability of personal computers, spread-sheets, statistical programs, and inexpensive data offered the opportunity to test indicators a bit more rigorously than by looking at a chart. Some proved worthy of further investigation; most did not pan out. The promising indicators formed the basis of a model for forecasting the stock market. In time, the model seemed to have too many variables. Moreover, some of the variables were difficult to justify. As a result, several were removed in favor of the five explanatory variables that follow. But first we will define the variable we are trying to predict in our stock market model.

THE FORECAST VARIABLE

We'll continue to use the total return on the Standard & Poor's Index of 500 common stocks, a widely used benchmark, as published by Ibbotson Associates. The forecast horizon will be six months. That is, based on data known through December 31, for example, the model will forecast the return from that date through June 30 of the next year.

One important adjustment is made to the **forecast variable.** The return on one-month Treasury bills (also published by Ibbotson), the so-called risk-free return, is subtracted from the total return on the S&P 500. The return on stocks less the risk-free return is called the excess return on stocks.

The use of the excess return on stocks has some advantages over the raw return on stocks. Suppose, for example, an investor has forecast that the total return on equities will be 15 percent in the coming year, several percentage points above the long-term compound annual average. Stocks look good, according to the forecast. Now consider that a 15 percent forecast could be made when Treasury bills are yielding 15 percent or 3 percent.

In the first instance, the investor has a choice between a risky asset with an expected return of 15 percent and a riskless asset with a certain return of 15 percent. Since stocks and Treasury bills have the same return potential and Treasury bills offer the return risk-free, many investors would favor Treasury bills. In the second instance, however, the expected return on stocks is significantly higher than the risk-free return, making stocks more attractive. By modeling the excess return on stocks, the return on stocks relative to the risk-free alternative is automatically taken into consideration. In symbols, the forecast variable is written as:

$$(S_6 / S_0) - (TB_6 / TB_0)$$

where S_6 and S_0 are values of the S&P 500 total return index six months after the current month and for the current month, respectively, and TB_6 and TB_0 are values of the one-month Treasury bill total return index for the same months.

THE PREDICTOR VARIABLES

Here are the predictor or X variables that will be used to forecast the excess return on stocks:

Predictor Variable 1: Dividend Yield We're back to our old friend. Since the forecast variable is the excess return on the S&P 500, this model uses the dividend yield on that index. High dividend yields are associated with good stock returns; low yields, with subpar stock returns. The dividend yield is calculated by dividing the current annualized payout on the S&P 500 by the price of the index itself, as published by Standard & Poor's. Each month's price is the average of the daily closing prices of the index for the month. In symbols, the dividend yield is

$$d_0 / P_0$$

where d_0 represents dividends and P_0 represents price, both as described above, for the current month.

Predictor Variable 2: 12-Month Percent Change in the Consumer Price Index for Urban Consumers (CPIU) This variable is the CPIU as published by the U.S. Department of Labor. Rising inflation generally erodes the value of financial assets. Given an upward shift in inflation, bond market investors require higher yields, sending bond prices lower. Higher yields make bonds relatively more attractive than stocks, limiting stock market returns. At the same time, when inflation rises, the Federal Reserve often responds by tightening monetary policy, sending short-term interest rates higher. Rising short rates can put a damper on economic activity, eventually sending corporate profits and stock prices lower. Rising inflation tends to be bad for stock prices; declining inflation, also called disinflation, is generally good for stock prices. The 12-month percent change is lagged one month—meaning that figures for one month are assumed to be known at the end of the following month—because, for example, inflation figures for November are released in December. In symbols this variable is written as:

$$(CPI_{-1}/CPI_{-13}) - 1$$

where CPI_{-1} and CPI_{-13} are levels of the Consumer Price Index 1 and 13 months previous to the current month, respectively.

Predictor Variable 3: 12-Month Change in the Credit Quality Spread The credit quality spread is defined as the difference between the yield on Baa and Aaa corporate bond yields, as published by Moody's Investors Service. The month's yield is an average of daily yields. The 12-month change for each month is calculated by starting with the credit quality spread for the current month and subtracting the credit quality spread from 12 months earlier. A widening credit quality spread means that investors require relatively more yield on lower quality bonds, indicating less confidence in the economy. But since stock prices typically trough some time shortly before the end of a recession, when confidence in the economy is at a cyclical low, widening credit spreads are associated with higher stock prices, a counterintuitive result. In symbols this variable is written:

$$(Baa_0 - Aaa_0) - (Baa_{-12} - Aaa_{-12})$$

where Baa_0 and Aaa_0 are Moody's corporate bond yields as described above in the current month and Baa_{-12} and Aaa_{-12} are the same corporate bond yields 12 months previous to the current month.

Predictor Variable 4: The Natural Logarithm of the 24-Month Price Return on the S&P 500 This variable is calculated by starting with the 24-month holding period return on the S&P 500, which equals the 24-month percent change in decimal form plus one. If the 24-month change in price were 10 percent (–10 percent), then the holding period return would be 1.10 (0.90). The variable is transformed one step further by taking the natural logarithm of the holding period return. Virtually all statistical packages and most spreadsheets will calculate the natural logarithm of any positive number; the natural logarithm of zero and negative numbers is undefined. The coefficient of this variable has a negative sign: Rising stock prices are generally followed by declining stock prices; and vice versa. The 24-month change in price was chosen in part because that time span is approximately one-half the duration of a typical economic cycle. The price for each month is the average of the daily S&P 500 closing prices. In symbols this variable is written:

$$ln(P_0/P_{-24})$$

where ln is the natural logarithm operator and P_0 and P_{-24} are prices of the S&P 500 as described above in the current month and 24 months previous to the current month, respectively.

Predictor Variable 5: Free Reserves This variable is the difference between two monetary aggregates published by the Federal Reserve Board: Excess Reserves and Borrowings of Depository

Institutions from the Federal Reserve. The amounts are monthly averages of daily figures in millions of dollars. The difference between the two aggregates, called free reserves, is an indicator of banking system liquidity. High levels of free reserves generally are followed by rising stock prices; a low or negative level of free reserves indicates the Federal Reserve is drawing liquidity out of the banking system and tends to send stock prices lower. In symbols this variable is simply

$$\text{Free}_0 / 1{,}000$$

where Free_0 is the level of free reserves as described above for the current month. The figure is divided by 1,000 solely as a matter of scaling convenience—this convention has a superficial affect on regression output and no affect on model forecasts.

REGRESSION OUTPUT AND ANALYSIS

Regression output for the period from 1964 through 1993 appears in Table 4–1. An initial scan of the output shows that each of the five predictor variables is significant—the weakest variable has a t-statistic of 6.18. The R-squared is 0.41, indicating that the five X variables explain 41 percent of the variation in six-month excess stock returns.

Note the introduction of the adjusted t-statistic in Table 4–1. This was added because the specification of the model created a problem. Recall that the variable Y being forecast is the six-month excess return estimated over the 30 years from 1964 through 1993. Since the data are monthly, they include 360 observations (12 months per year times 30 years).

The problem is that the 360 observations are not independent. The six-month excess return from January through June 1964 is highly correlated with the six-month excess return from February through July 1964. These two observations have five months in common. Since the forecast interval is six months, there are really only 60 independent observations (two per year times 30 years).

T A B L E   4-1

Regression Output for the Stock Market Model*

Constant	−0.11
Standard error of Y estimate	0.09
R-squared	0.41
Number of observations	360

	Dividend Yield	12-Month Change CPIU	12-Month Change Credit Spread	Log 2-Year Change S&P 500	Free Reserves
	X_1	X_2	X_3	X_4	X_5
X-coefficient	0.07	−2.03	0.09	−0.18	0.05
Standard error of X-coefficient	0.01	0.25	0.01	0.03	0.01
T-statistic	9.91	−8.19	6.65	−6.28	6.18
Adjusted t-statistic	4.05	−3.34	2.71	−2.56	2.52

*The forecast variable is the six-month excess stock return. The estimation period is from 1964 through 1993.

Sources:

Y: © Stocks, Bonds, Bills, and Inflation 1996 Yearbook™, Ibbotson Associates, Chicago (annually updates work by Roger G. Ibbotson and Rex A. Sinquefield). Used with permission. All rights reserved;

X_1, X_4: Standard & Poor's. Used with permission of Standard & Poor's, a division of the McGraw-Hill Companies;

X_3: Moody's Investors Service (used with permission);

X_5: Federal Reserve Board.

Recall that the t-statistic is calculated by dividing the X-coefficient by the standard error of the X-coefficient. The standard error of the X-coefficient turns out to be directly related to the square root of the number of observations in the regression. As the number of observations increases, the standard error of the X-coefficient declines, increasing the magnitude of the t-statistic as a result.

In our model, the regression process "sees" 360 observations, but there are only 60 independent observations. The adjusted t-statistic corrects this problem by dividing the reported t-statistic by the square root of six.[9]

TABLE 4–2

Summary Output for Six Subregressions*

	Coefficients				
	X_1	X_2	X_3	X_4	X_5
Jan/Jul	0.07	−2.15	0.13	−0.14	0.06
Feb/Aug	0.05	−1.39	0.05	−0.18	0.06
Mar/Sep	0.09	−2.89	0.07	−0.24	0.02
Apr/Oct	0.07	−2.12	0.11	−0.14	0.04
May/Nov	0.09	−2.25	0.10	−0.18	0.05
Jun/Dec	0.07	−1.92	0.10	−0.24	0.08
Averages	0.07	−2.12	0.09	−0.19	0.05
	T-statistics				
	X_1	X_2	X_3	X_4	X_5
Jan/Jul	4.15	−3.94	3.71	−2.05	3.00
Feb/Aug	3.26	−2.54	1.69	−2.51	3.18
Mar/Sep	4.10	−3.79	1.79	−2.78	0.66
Apr/Oct	4.37	−3.63	3.84	−2.04	2.00
May/Nov	4.55	−3.62	3.08	−2.44	2.71
Jun/Dec	3.96	−2.76	2.28	−3.21	3.69
Averages	4.07	−3.38	2.73	−2.50	2.54

*Breaking up the original regression eliminates the problem of overlapping data. Notice that the *t*-statistics drop sharply but generally are still statistically significant. Average values for the coefficients are close to those of the full regression reported in Table 4–1. Average values for the *t*-statistics also are close to the adjusted *t*-statistics reported in Table 4–1.

There is another way to approach the overlapping observation problem. We can look at the full 360-observation regression as six subregressions, each with 60 observations. The first subregression includes the 30 years of January and July observations; the second, the February and August observations; and so on.

Summary data for these six subregressions are shown in Table 4–2. Average values for the coefficients are approximately

T A B L E   4–3

Pairwise Correlation Matrix for the Five Predictor or X-Variables Used for the Regression in Table 4–1

	Dividend Yield	12-Month Change CPIU	12-Month Change Credit Spread	Log 2-Year Change S&P 500	Free Reserves
	X_1	X_2	X_3	X_4	X_5
X_1	1.00				
X_2	0.70	1.00			
X_3	0.28	0.48	1.00		
X_4	−0.32	−0.42	−0.40	1.00	
X_5	−0.43	−0.55	−0.14	.033	1.00

Sources: X_1, X_4: Standard & Poor's. Used with permission of Standard & Poor's, a division of the McGraw-Hill Companies; X_2: U.S. Department of Labor; X_3: Moody's Investors Service (used with permission); X_5: Federal Reserve Board.

equal to those of the regression reported in Table 4–1. The average values for the t-statistics are approximately equal to the adjusted t-statistics reported in Table 4–1.

The adjusted t-statistic is important because overlapping observations in a regression model inflate the reported t-statistics. Predictor variables with significant t-statistics may in fact be insignificant when the adjustment for the number of independent observations is taken into consideration.

Now we consider whether any of the correlations among the explanatory variables are exceedingly high. First we look at the correlation matrix shown in Table 4–3. The highest correlation is between the dividend yield and the 12-month change in the CPIU. The value, 0.70, falls below the danger level of 0.85 discussed in Chapter 3, so pairwise correlations are not a problem.

TABLE 4–4

Multiple R and R-Squared Measures for Five Regressions*

Regression	Multiple R	R-Squared
X_1 vs. X_2, X_3, X_4, and X_5	0.70	0.49
X_2 vs. X_1, X_3, X_4, and X_5	0.81	0.65
X_3 vs. X_1, X_2, X_4, and X_5	0.57	0.32
X_4 vs. X_1, X_2, X_3, and X_5	0.50	0.25
X_5 vs. X_1, X_2, X_3, and X_4	0.58	0.34

*X_1 versus X_2, X_3, X_4, and X_5; X_2 versus X_1, X_3, X_4, and X_5; and so on. None of the multiple Rs exceed 0.85, the critical level cited in Chapter 3.

Sources:X_1, X_4: Standard & Poor's. Used with permission of Standard & Poor's, a division of the McGraw-Hill Companies; X_2: U.S. Department of Labor; X_3: Moody's Investors Service (used with permission); X_5: Federal Reserve Board.

As we discussed in Chapter 3, however, reviewing only the pairwise correlations does not eliminate the possibility that one predictor variable is highly correlated with two or more of the other predictor variables. To check for this possibility, we run one regression for each of the five explanatory variables: X_1 against X_2, X_3, X_4, and X_5; X_2 against X_1, X_3, X_4, and X_5; and so on. The multiple R and R-squared measures are shown in Table 4–4. None of the multiple Rs exceed 0.85, the critical level cited in Chapter 3.

Now we will consider whether any of the five X variables have any influence points. The idea, discussed in Chapter 3 and shown graphically in Figure 3–1, is to eliminate the possibility that the information in each of the independent variables has not been influenced by one or a few points. If 90 percent of a variable's information is contained in one or two observations, then an analyst arguably might have little confidence that a current observation used to make a forecast would contain any useful information. In such a case the variable in question should be removed from the model unless there are theoretical or otherwise compelling reasons for leaving the variable in the model. If an otherwise good predictor variable has a distorting outlier, one solution is simply to remove the offending observation when estimating the model.

We start the search for influence points by running a regression of Y, the forecast variable, against four of the five explanatory variables. Using the regression output, we create the residuals. (An example showing the calculation of residuals appears in Appendix 1.) Then we plot the residuals, which contain the variation in Y left unexplained by the four X-variables in question, against the fifth explanatory variable and scan the plot for influence points. We repeat this procedure, which can be done easily by some statistical software programs, for each of the five explanatory variables.

Influence plots, which appear for the first two predictor variables of the model in Figure 4–1, indicate whether removal of any one point would change the model meaningfully. None of the charts showed the existence of any influence points. The charts also are useful because they show how much explanatory power, on the margin, is added by each predictor variable relative to the other four. Finally, searches for influence points can help in ferreting out bad data points, since a bad data point often appears on the plot as an extreme outlier.

Now we will consider trying to improve the model by examining the residual, or error terms. Recall the fourth assumption of the classical linear regression model: There is no relationship between successive error terms; in other words, the error terms are not correlated. Rather than considering correlated error terms a liability, however, we will try to turn any correlation found into an asset. The idea is that any pattern in the error terms might be used to improve the model's forecasts. For example, if a positive error tends to be followed by another positive error, that tendency could be used to make a better prediction of the forecast variable.

F I G U R E   4–1

Looking for Influence Points

The first chart plots the residuals from the regression Y versus X_2, X_3, X_4, and X_5 against X_1. The second chart plots the residuals from the regression Y versus X_1, X_3, X_4, and X_5 against X_2. The zeros indicate that for the plots shown, removal of a single point would not change the corrlation meaningfully. The process for each of X_3, X_4, and X_5 also showed that there were no influence points.

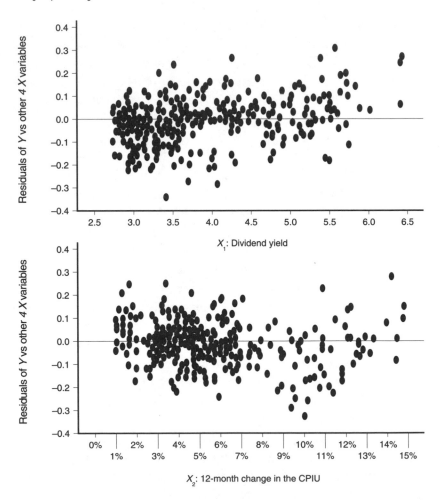

Sources: © *Stocks, Bonds, Bills, and Inflation 1996 Yearbook™*, Ibbotson Associates, Chicago (annually updates work by Roger G. Ibbotson and Rex A. Sinquefield). Used with permission. All rights reserved.
Used with permission of Standard & Poor's, a division of the McGraw-Hill Companies; U.S. Department of Labor.

One way to look for a pattern is to calculate the correlation between each residual and the residual from the previous observation. Note that this analysis will have one less observation since there is no observation before the first observation. If the correlation is positive, meaning that positive errors tend to follow positive errors and negatives tend to follow negatives, then the residuals are said to exhibit *positive serial correlation*. Less frequently, negative serial correlation will occur, meaning the error terms have a tendency to reverse from positive to negative and vice versa.

Another way to test for first-order serial correlation is to look at what is called the **Durbin-Watson (DW) statistic,** which is calculated by many statistical software packages. Using the DW statistic is better than looking at the correlations between adjacent residuals because the serial correlation could be the result of serial correlation of the predictor variables. The DW test statistic helps to distinguish the source of the serial correlation.

The Durbin-Watson statistic falls in a range between zero and four. If there is no first-order serial correlation, the DW statistic will be about two. If there is positive serial correlation, the DW statistic will be less than two; a DW statistic greater than two means there is negative serial correlation.

Regression output including the Durbin-Watson statistic for our stock model appears in Table 4–5. The reported DW statistic is 0.58, sharply less than two, indicating strong positive serial correlation of the error terms. Unfortunately, the overlapping data that inflated the reported *t*-statistics deflates the Durbin-Watson statistic. Since successive *Y*-variable observations are correlated, so are the residuals.

Once again, in order to get a better read on the DW statistic, we break the regression into the six subregressions, each of which has independent observations of the forecast variable. The data summarized in Table 4–6 show an average DW statistic of 2.50, reversing the initial finding and actually indicating the presence of negative first-order serial correlation of the error terms.

TABLE 4–5

Regression Output for the Stock Market Model Including the Durbin-Watson Statistic*

Constant	−0.11
Standard error of Y estimate	0.09
R-squared	0.41
Number of observations	360
Durbin-Watson statistic	0.58

	Dividend Yield	12-Month Change CPIU	12-Month Change Credit Spread	Log 2-Year Change S&P 500	Free Reserves
	X_1	X_2	X_3	X_4	X_5
X-coefficient	0.07	−2.03	0.09	−0.18	0.05
Standard error of X-coefficient	0.01	0.25	0.01	0.03	0.01
T-statistic	9.91	−8.19	6.65	−6.28	6.18
Adjusted T-statistic	4.05	−3.34	2.71	−2.56	2.52

*The estimation period is from 1964 through 1993.

Sources: Y: © Stocks, Bonds, Bills, and Inflation 1996 Yearbook™, Ibbotson Associates, Chicago (annually updates work by Roger G. Ibbotson and Rex A. Sinquefield). Used with permission. All rights reserved;
X_1, X_4: Standard & Poor's. Used with permission of Standard & Poor's, a division of the McGraw-Hill Companies;
X_2: U.S. Department of Labor;
X_3: Moody's Investors Service (used with permission);
X_5: Federal Reserve Board.

Two questions follow. First, is the negative serial correlation indicated by the Durbin-Watson statistic statistically significant? And second, if it is, how do we take advantage of the information to improve our forecasts?

According to the work published by Durbin and Watson in the early 1950s, we need to consider the number of observations in the regression (60) and the X-variables (5) to determine whether the DW statistic for the model is signaling statistically

TABLE 4–6

Durbin-Watson Statistics for the Six Subregressions*

	Durbin-Watson Statistic
Jan/Jul	2.52
Feb/Aug	2.48
Mar/Sep	2.22
Apr/Oct	2.55
May/Nov	2.50
Jun/Dec	2.73
Average	2.50

*The subregressions eliminate the overlapping data problem that deflated the Durbin-Watson statistic to a level sharply below two, initially indicating positive serial correlation. Adjusted for the overlapping data, the residuals actually exhibit negative first-order serial correlation since the DW statistics for the subregressions are consistently above two.

significant negative serial correlation. Data from a table published by Durbin and Watson indicate that a value of 2.59 is needed to conclude that negative serial correlation is present with 95 percent certainty. Our value, 2.50, falls in the upper end of a gray area (between 2.26 and 2.59) for concluding that negative serial correlation is present.[10]

We will proceed on the assumption that negative serial correlation is present and try to use the information to improve the forecast despite the fact that the DW statistic fell in the gray indeterminate area. One reason for this assumption is that the presence of a previous value of Y as an explanatory variable tends to deflate the Durbin-Watson statistic. Although we are not using a lagged value of Y as an explanatory variable, the model does have the 24-month change in the stock market, which is correlated to the forecast variable, the six-month excess return of the stock market. So it is possible that the Durbin-Watson statistic is lower than it otherwise would be. In any case, since the DW statistic is in the upper range of the gray area for concluding that negative serial correlation is present, it won't hurt to try to take advantage of the condition to improve the model.

The process that incorporates the information from the residuals into the forecast is called first-order autoregressive correction or AR(1). It was first proposed by Cochrane and Orcutt in 1949, so the procedure is also known by their names. The process is not trivial but thankfully, many statistics packages can do it.

The AR(1) or Cochrane-Orcutt procedure is an iterative process. First, a normal regression is run. The residuals are computed and the correlation between adjacent residuals is examined to create a forecast of each residual from its previous value. This information about the residuals is incorporated into a second regression which offers a second set of residuals and a second estimate of the correlation between adjacent residuals. The process continues until the estimate of how the residuals are correlated does not change meaningfully.[11]

Once again we will look at both the full regression model and the six subregressions. For the subregressions we will add the AR(1) process. We will add an AR(6) process to the full model, because it has a six-month forecast horizon. The AR(6) process will allow us to incorporate how each residual is correlated to the residual from the observation six months back. The new regression output, which appears in Tables 4–7 and 4–8, shows that the AR process eliminated the autocorrelation of the error terms (the DW statistics fell to approximately two) and increased the explanatory power of the model.

As we come to the close of this chapter, it is well worth noting that largely the same or perhaps better results could be achieved with different, more, or even fewer variables than we proposed here for forecasting the stock market. The predictor variables were chosen to capture monetary policy (free reserves), value (dividend yield), investor sentiment (credit spread), and the economic cycle (24-month change in stock prices). Inflation is a multifaceted variable: it is of concern to monetary authorities;

T A B L E   4–7

Regression Output for the Stock Market Model Including the AR(6) Term*

Constant		−0.09			
Standard error of Y estimate		0.08			
R-squared		0.47			
Number of observations		360			
Durbin-Watson statistic		0.54			

	Dividend Yield	12-Month Change CPIU	12-Month Change Credit Spread	Log 2-Year Change S&P 500	Free Reserves
	X_1	X_2	X_3	X_4	X_5
X-coefficient	0.06	−1.67	0.10	−0.13	0.06
Standard error of X-coefficient	0.01	0.19	0.01	0.02	0.01
T-statistic	11.01	−8.73	8.78	−5.52	8.99
Adjusted t-Statistic	4.49	−3.56	3.59	−2.25	3.67
	AR(6)				
X-coefficient	−0.34				
Standard error of X-coefficient	0.05				
T-statistic	−6.33				
Adjusted t-statistic	−2.58				

*The estimation period is from 1964 through 1993. Notice that the addition of the AR(6) term increases the R-squared measure from 0.41 to 0.47. The Durbin-Watson Statistic remains skewed by the overlapping data.

Sources: Y: © *Stocks, Bonds, Bills, and Inflation 1996 Yearbook™*, Ibbotson Associates, Chicago (annually updates work by Roger G. Ibbotson and Rex A. Sinquefield). Used with permission. All rights reserved;
X_1, X_4: Standard & Poor's. Used with permission of Standard & Poor's, a division of the McGraw-Hill Companies;
X_2: U.S. Department of Labor;
X_3: Moody's Investors Service (used with permission);
X_5: Federal Reserve Board.

relative to the dividend yield it says something about value; it also affects sentiment and says something about where we are in the economic cycle. Clearly other economic or market-related data might better forecast the stock market. For example, some combination of monetary aggregates or interest rates might dominate the explanatory power of free reserves.

TABLE 4–8

Regression Output for the Six Subregressions Including the Durbin-Watson Statistic and R-Squared Measure*

	X_1	X_2	X_3	X_4	X_5	DW Statistic	R-Squared
Jan/Jul							
X-coefficient	0.07	−2.15	0.12	−0.14	0.06	2.52	0.48
T-statistic	4.15	−3.94	3.71	−2.05	3.00		
Feb/Aug							
X-coefficient	0.05	−1.39	0.05	−0.18	0.06	2.48	0.38
T-statistic	3.26	−2.54	1.69	−2.51	3.18		
Mar/Sep							
X-coefficient	0.09	−2.89	0.07	−0.24	0.02	2.22	0.37
T-statistic	4.10	−3.79	1.79	−2.78	0.66		
Apr/Oct							
X-coefficient	0.07	−2.12	0.11	−0.14	0.04	2.55	0.47
T-statistic	4.37	−3.63	3.84	−2.04	2.00		
May/Nov							
X-coefficient	0.09	−2.25	0.10	−0.18	0.05	2.50	0.49
T-statistic	4.55	−3.62	3.08	−2.44	2.71		
Jun/Dec							
X-coefficient	0.07	−1.92	0.10	−0.24	0.08	2.73	0.47
T-statistic	3.96	−2.76	2.28	−3.21	3.69		
Averages	0.07	−2.12	0.09	−0.19	0.05	2.50	0.44
	4.07	3.38	3.73	2.50	2.54		

	X_1	X_2	X_3	X_4	X_5	AR(1)	DW Statistic	R-Squared
Jan/Jul								
X-coefficient	0.06	−1.85	0.01	−0.13	0.07	−0.30	1.97	0.52
T-statistic	4.90	−4.17	4.11	−2.34	4.31	−2.22		
Feb/Aug								
X-coefficient	0.05	−1.20	0.07	−0.14	0.07	−0.30	2.03	0.43
T-statistic	3.83	−2.71	2.36	−2.25	4.23	−2.13		
Mar/Sep								
X-coefficient	0.07	−2.14	0.09	−0.16	0.04	−0.30	2.09	0.39
T-statistic	3.85	−3.22	2.51	−1.98	1.65	−1.94		
Apr/Oct								
X-coefficient	0.06	−1.62	0.12	−0.08	0.05	−0.39	2.13	0.53
T-statistic	4.85	−3.66	5.21	−1.39	3.38	−2.91		

TABLE   4–8

Regression Output for the Six Subregressions Including the Durbin-Watson Statistic and R-Squared Measure* *(concluded)*

	X_1	X_2	X_3	X_4	X_5	AR(1)	DW Statistic	R-Squared
May/Nov								
X-coefficient	0.07	−1.79	0.10	−0.13	0.05	−0.33	1.98	0.53
T-statistic	4.78	−3.60	3.63	−2.09	3.61	−2.33		
Jun/Dec								
X-coefficient	0.06	−1.64	0.11	−0.18	0.08	−0.44	2.09	0.56
T-statistic	4.78	−3.30	3.46	−3.07	5.08	−3.32		
Averages								
X-coefficient	0.06	−1.71	0.08	−0.13	0.06	−0.34	2.05	0.49
T-statistic	4.50	−3.44	3.55	−2.19	3.71	−2.48		

*In the first output table, the DW statistic averages 2.50, indicating the existence of negative first-order autocorrelation of error terms. The second output table shows the effect of the AR term, the addition of which reduced the average DW statistic to 2.05. The elimination of the negative autocorrelation increased the average R-squared from 0.44 to 0.49.

Sources: *Y:* © *Stocks, Bonds, Bills, and Inflation 1996 Yearbook™*, Ibbotson Associates, Chicago (annually updates work by Roger G. Ibbotson and Rex A. Sinquefield). Used with permission. All rights reserved;
X_1, X_4: Standard & Poor's. Used with permission of Standard & Poor's, a division of the McGraw-Hill Companies;
X_2: U.S. Department of Labor;
X_3: Moody's Investors Service (used with permission);
X_5: Federal Reserve Board.

Experience shows, however, that new variables or variations on existing variables often do not lift the explanatory power of a model. The variables proposed here often contain virtually all of the useful information any new variable has to offer. It is almost as if there were a wall of random noise in stock prices that is extremely difficult to hurdle. Nevertheless, it is probably true that any model can be improved, although it often turns out to be easier said than done.

Many analysts prefer the natural logarithm of the holding period return over the percent change as the forecast variable for a stock market model. That's because theory holds that stock price changes are log-normally distributed, that is, changes cal culated using the log function are normally distributed (a distri- bution plot of the changes would be shaped like the famous bell curve). The problem is that the variable using the logarithm func- tion does not appear to be "more normal" than the percent change configuration. Indeed, for the 60 six-month periods from 1964 through 1993, excess stock returns turn out to be approxi- mately normal whether measured as percent returns or as the log of holding period returns. So the additional step of using the log of the forecast variable and then "untransforming" the forecasts back to a percent return figure does not appear to be worth the trouble and probably would not improve the model's forecasts.

Another possible change: Why not try to forecast the next month's excess return rather than the six-month excess return? Why go through all the trouble with the overlapping data? The reason is that the explanatory variables were chosen with a longer horizon in mind. Intuitively, a model designed to fore- cast the next month's excess return would have faster acting explanatory variables than the predictor variables for a model with a six-month horizon. For example, the one-month percent change in the Consumer Price Index might be used rather than the 12-month percent change to forecast the next month's excess return on the stock market. As it turns out, however, measures of shorter-term changes in economic variables are often unreli- able. Hence, the use of longer horizons for both the forecast and predictor variables.

CHAPTER

5

A BOND
MARKET MODEL

I have often thought that the bond market is more difficult to forecast than the stock market. Ask any Wall Street strategist what single most important factor drives the stock market and the answer is likely to be the "monetary environment" or simply "interest rates." If stock market strategists can hang their hats on interest rates, then what is the appropriate equivalent factor for bond market strategists?

In the late 1980s I began looking for the bond market Holy Grail, and of course, I didn't find it. I did find one article particularly helpful in thinking about bonds. What's more, analysis of the article offered ideas regarding potential predictor variables for a model designed to forecast the bond market. Now, although I found the article useful, the more important reason for mentioning it is to suggest that analysts should not be shy about "grazing" the research for ideas. Typically, however, ideas alone cannot be put into a model; they must be distilled in order to synthesize promising predictor variables. Readers will immediately observe that the title of the article that drew my attention was designed perfectly for that purpose.

"A Bond Market Timing Model," written by Yoav Benari, appeared in the Fall 1988 issue of *The Journal of Portfolio Management*. Right off the bat the article explores the difference between owning a short- or long-term bond. The quick answer is that a short-term bond owner is guaranteed principle on relatively short notice and a long-term bond holder is guaranteed a certain level of income over an extended period of time. Neither investor is guaranteed both of these distinct investment characteristics.

A long-term bondholder who sells before maturity may suffer a loss of principle if interest rates rise. According to Benari, "there exists some 'normal' positive risk premium, relating long- to short-term bonds, which reflects [this] risk of an unanticipated shortening of the investor's holding period." The normal risk premium is driven by two factors. First, it is positively related to bond market volatility, since heightened bond market volatility increases the odds of a large increase in yields and a large loss of principle. The second factor is the potential for inflation to accelerate, which also is positively related to the normal risk premium, since accelerating inflation also could lead to higher interest rates and a large loss of principle.

The "observed" risk premium is the actual yield on long-term bonds relative to inflation expectations. Benari suggests that the five-year annualized rate of inflation be used as a proxy for inflation expectations, so the observed risk premium is simply the long-term bond yield less the five-year annualized rate of inflation.

The difference between the normal and observed risk premiums is what offers the opportunity to time the bond market. When the observed risk premium exceeds the normal risk premium, creating a positive *excess* risk premium, then investors have sent bond yields too high (or bond prices too low) and long-term bonds are likely to outperform short-term bonds. When the observed risk premium is less than the normal risk premium, just the opposite has occurred, and short-term bonds are likely to out-perform long-term bonds. In symbols, we can write:

$$P_x = P_o - P_n \qquad (1)$$

where

P_x is the excess risk premium,
P_o is the observed risk premium, and
P_n is the normal risk premium.

Now, as we said earlier, the normal risk premium P_n depends on bond market volatility and inflation acceleration. In symbols, we can write:

$$P_n = f_1(\text{vol}) + f_2(\text{acc}) \qquad (2)$$

where $f_1(\text{vol})$ is a function of bond market volatility and $f_2(\text{acc})$ is a function of inflation acceleration.

Now, if we substitute P_n as described in Equation (2) into Equation (1), then we get:

$$P_x = P_o - f_1(\text{vol}) - f_2(\text{acc})$$

Finally, if we recall that P_o is the long-term bond yield less the five-year inflation rate (the "real" interest rate) then we get:

$$P_x = \text{Real} - f_1(\text{vol}) - f_2(\text{acc})$$

We now have the basis for testing a model to forecast the bond market. When P_x, the excess risk premium is high, then long-term bonds are supposed to outperform short-term bonds. In order for this to occur the real interest rate (Real) needs to be high rather than low and both bond market volatility (vol) and the tendency for inflation to accelerate (acc) need to be low rather than high. In terms of a regression model with bond returns as the forecast variable, we would expect the coefficient of the variable Real to be positive and the other two coefficients to be negative.

An empirical test of the above variables yielded results that were largely in line with expectations. The real interest rate variable (Real) had a strongly positive coefficient. The bond market volatility (vol) variable had a negative sign, but it was only weakly positive, so the variable was dropped from the model.[12] Inflation acceleration variables tested (acc) were indeterminate, but a lagged inflation variable was apparently very successful in capturing the acceleration phenomenon. Details of the model, which includes additional variables as well, follow.

THE FORECAST VARIABLE

There are two basic ways to specify the forecast variable for a bond market model. One way is to forecast bond yields, that is, interest rates; the other, bond market total returns. We will argue in favor of forecasting total returns and proceed to present a model in which the forecast variable is based on the total return concept. Of course, some analysts nevertheless may prefer to model interest rates.

As shown in Table 5–1, changes in yield are not linearly related to total returns on bonds. Consider, for example, a 30-year Treasury bond issued at a price of 100 with a 10 percent coupon. If interest rates were 1.5 percentage points below the initial rate at the close of the first year of issue, the total return on the bond would be 26.1 percent. A 1.5 percentage point rise, however, would result in a total return of –2.5 percent. The lopsided return differential is due in part to the guaranteed 10 percent annual interest income that adds to price gains when interest rates fall and cushions declines in price when interest rates rise. Also, as shown in Table 5–1, the price return on a bond is not symmetric with respect to an equal but opposite change in yield. A 1.5 percentage point drop results in a 16.1 percent gain in price; a 1.5 percent percentage point rise, however, results in a 12.5 percent price decline. A second complicating factor is that total returns on bonds depend on the level of interest rates at

TABLE 5-1

Comparing Changes in Yield to Total Return on a 30-Year Treasury Bond Issued at Par (initial price = 100.0)

Case One: Yield on Issue is 10%

Yield One Year Hence	Change in Yield	Price One Year Hence	Price Return	Coupon Return	Total Return
8.5%	−1.5%	116.1	16.1%	10.0%	26.1%
9.0	−1.0	110.2	10.2	10.0	20.2
9.5	−0.5	104.9	4.9	10.0	14.9
10.0	0.0	100.0	0.0	10.0	10.0
10.5	0.5	95.5	−4.5	10.0	5.5
11.0	1.0	91.3	−8.7	10.0	1.3
11.5	1.5	87.5	−12.5	10.0	−2.5

Case Two: Yield on Issue is 7%

Yield One Year Hence	Change in Yield	Price One Year Hence	Price Return	Coupon Return	Total Return
5.5%	−1.5%	121.6	21.6%	7.0%	28.6%
6.0	−1.0	113.7	13.7	7.0	20.7
6.5	−0.5	106.5	6.5	7.0	13.5
7.0	0.0	100.0	0.0	7.0	7.0
7.5	0.5	94.1	-5.9	7.0	1.1
8.0	1.0	88.8	−11.2	7.0	−4.2
8.5	1.5	83.9	−16.1	7.0	−9.1

the beginning of the measuring period. If there is no change in interest rates, the return on a bond yielding 10 percent is about 10 percent over a year's time; the 7 percent bond, meanwhile, would return about 7 percent.

Assuming an analyst chooses to forecast interest rates, each yield forecast would have to be translated into a return forecast. After all, changes in yield do not go into an investor's pocket book; rather the return is the combined effect of bond price changes and interest income. By choosing total return as the forecast variable, the need for transformations is avoided.

Even if we agree to forecast total return, however, many choices remain. For example, major brokerage houses track several bond indexes. The data, however, typically go back only to the early 1970s. The broad-based bond indexes, moreover, have another problem: Their composition drifts over time, in part because issuers prefer to issue longer-term bonds at some times and shorter-term bonds at other times. As a result, the average maturity of broad-based bond indexes drifts, making their sensitivity to interest rate fluctuations variable over time.

Fortunately, some excellent monthly return data published by Ibbotson Associates are available for long-term Treasury issues going back to the late 1920s. The return series is by no means perfect, owing to changing Treasury issuance practices over time, but it is about as good as it can get.

As was the case for the stock market model, this model will forecast a six-month excess return, the six-month excess return on long-term government bonds. That is, the forecast variable will be the six-month return on long-term governments less the six-month return on one-month Treasury bills, as published by Ibbotson Associates. In symbols, the forecast variable can be written as

$$(B_6 / B_0) - (TB_6 / TB_0)$$

where B_6 and B_0 are values of the Ibbotson long-term government bond total return index for six months after the current month and for the current month, respectively, and TB_6 and TB_0 are values of the Ibbotson one-month Treasury bill total return index for the same months. The actual long-term bonds used by Ibbotson are Treasury issues with a maturity of approximately 20 years.

THE PREDICTOR VARIABLES

Here are the predictor variables the model will use to forecast the excess return on long-term government bonds:

Predictor Variable 1: The Real Interest Rate   The real interest rate is the yield on a bond less the expected rate of inflation. Excluding the effect of taxes, the real rate of return indicates how much an investment's buying power increases. As with most economic concepts, however, the definition is in the eye of the beholder. The Federal Reserve Board's Long Term Treasury Composite Yield, which is published monthly and dates back to 1947, serves as the yield portion of the real interest rate. This yield is a monthly average of daily figures. Following Benari's lead, we will use the five-year annualized rate of inflation, as measured by the Consumer Price Index for Urban Consumers, as our estimate of inflation expectations. Since there is a one-month lag in the release of the inflation data—figures for January are released in February, for example—the five-year inflation rate through the previous month is subtracted from the long-term Treasury bond yield for the current month to calculate the real interest rate for the current month. In symbols this variable can be written as:

$$LTT_0 - ((CPI_{-1} / CPI_{-61})^{.2} - 1)$$

where LTT_0 is the Long Term Treasury Composite yield (expressed as a decimal) in the current month and CPI_{-1} and CPI_{-61} are levels of the Consumer Price Index one and 61 months previous to the current month. The superscript .2 is an exponent and is equivalent to taking the fifth root of the ratio of the CPI levels.

As an alternative to Benari's analysis, we can think of the real interest rate as an indicator of value for bonds just as the dividend yield was considered an indicator of value for stocks. When real interest rates are high, a bondholder has a cushion between the nominal return on a bond and the level of inflation. Thus, when real interest rates are high, the bondholder enjoys a higher probability that the buying power of the investment will not diminish. Likewise, when real interest rates are low, a modest increase in inflation damages the buying power of an investment in bonds.

There is a problem, of course, in using an historical inflation rate as a proxy for future inflation. High real interest rates,
for example, could be followed by sharply higher inflation, eras-
ing the implied cushion of the high real interest rate. Even so,
the real interest rate, as defined above, is positively correlated
with future excess returns on bonds; that is, high real interest
rates are associated with good excess bond returns and low real
rates with poor excess bond returns.

Predictor Variable 2: A Lagged Measure of Inflation   Here we use
the four-year inflation rate lagged one year, which is calculated
by dividing the Consumer Price Index lagged 61 months by the
Consumer Price Index lagged 13 months. Note that since the
earlier level of the CPI is the numerator of the fraction, we are
really looking at the reciprocal of a lagged measure of inflation.
The variable is slow moving and complements the real interest
rate variable, which has as a component the most recent annualized five-year change in the Consumer Price Index. Indeed,
including a form of both the five-year inflation rate and a lagged
four-year inflation rate allows the regression model in some
respects to "see" whether inflation is accelerating. In symbols,
this variable is written:

$$CPI_{-61} / CPI_{-13}$$

where CPI_{-61} and CPI_{-13} are levels of the Consumer Price Index 61
and 13 months previous to the current month, respectively.

Predictor Variable 3: The Two-Year Total Return on the S&P 500   This
variable is an indicator of future economic activity. Rising stock
prices are associated with a pickup in economic activity, which
causes businesses and consumers to increase their borrowing.
The resultant lift in the demand for capital leads to higher interest rates, a negative for future bond returns. Alternatively, the
increase in economic activity that follows rising stock prices
causes demand for goods and labor to rise. Upward pressure on

wages and prices (inflation) follows as a result, also a negative for bond prices. In symbols, this variable can be written as

$$(P_0 / P_{-24}) - 1$$

where P_0 and P_{-24} are values for a total return index on the S&P 500 in the current month and 24 months previous to the current month, respectively.

Predictor Variable 4: The Six-Month Total Return on Treasury Bills Rising short-term rates often signal future economic strength, rising inflation expectations, or both, which can lead to higher long-term rates, a negative for bond returns. This variable symbolically is represented as:

$$(TB_0 / TB_{-6}) - 1$$

where TB_0 and TB_{-6} are values of a total return index on one-month Treasury bills in the current month and six months previous to the current month, respectively.

Predictor Variable 5: The 12-Month Percent Change in Oil and Gold Stock Prices This variable is calculated as the average of the 12-month percent changes in oil and gold stocks as measured by Standard & Poor's. The indexes measure price only—they are not total return indexes—and figures used are daily closes at month's end. Since oil and gold prices are linked to future rates of inflation, a rise in this variable is associated with poor bond returns; a decline in the variable, with good bond returns.

The use of oil and gold stock prices, rather than the underlying prices of oil and gold, warrants some discussion. The idea is that prices of oil and gold stocks better reflect the market's view of the future price of oil and gold than do the prices of the underlying commodities. Oil and gold prices often fluctuate due to short-term swings in supply and demand that the stock market takes into consideration when pricing oil and gold stocks. During the Gulf war and the crisis that preceded it, for example, the price of oil shot up sharply, but oil stocks barely budged, perhaps indicating that the price spike was going to be temporary. On the other hand, oil stocks rose sharply in the 1970s when rising oil prices were not thought to be a temporary phenomenon. In symbols, this variable can be written as:

$$\frac{((Gold_0 / Gold_{-12})-1) + ((Oil_0 / Oil_{-12})-1)}{2}$$

where $Gold_0$ and $Gold_{-12}$ are month-end gold stock prices as described above in the current month and 12 months previous to the current month, respectively, and likewise for Oil_0 and Oil_{-12}.

REGRESSION OUTPUT AND ANALYSIS

Table 5–2 shows the regression output for the bond model. As in the stock model, the forecast horizon is six months and the estimation period is the 30 years from 1964 through 1993. The R-squared is 0.42, meaning that the model explains 42 percent of the squared variation of the six-month excess bond returns. All of the t-statistics, adjusted for the overlapping data, are significant.

As in the stock market model discussed in Chapter 4, the low Durbin-Watson statistic incorrectly implies that the error terms are positively autocorrelated, a result of the use of overlapping data. The average Durbin-Watson statistic for the six subregressions, shown at the bottom of Table 5–2, is 2.14, however, well below the 2.23 cutoff value for indeterminacy suggested by Durbin and Watson. Thus, no attempt will be made to improve the model by way of an error correction process.

The pairwise correlation matrix for the five predictor variables is shown in Table 5-3. Only one correlation, between the lagged inflation variable and the six-month total return on Treasury bills, is meaningfully high. But the multicollinearity test, also shown in Table 5–3, indicates that none of the multiple Rs exceeds 0.85, the critical level discussed in Chapter 3. Hence, multicollinearity is not a problem in this model.

T A B L E   5–2

Regression Output for the Bond Market Model*

Constant	3.92
Standard error of Y estimate	0.06
R-squared	0.42
Number of observations	360
Durbin-Watson statistic	0.46

	Real Interest Rate	Lagged Inflation	Log 2-Year Return S&P 500	6-Month T-Bill Return	12-Month Change Oil and Gold Stocks
	X_1	X_2	X_3	X_4	X_5
X-coefficient	0.03	−0.70	−0.11	−3.12	−0.06
Standard error of X-coefficient	0.00	0.07	0.02	0.40	0.01
T-statistic	12.72	−10.30	−6.64	−7.87	−5.00
Adjusted T-statistic	5.19	−4.21	−2.71	−3.21	−2.04

Subregression Output

	Jan/Jul	Feb/Aug	Mar/Sep	Apr/Oct	May/Nov	Jun/Dec
Durbin-Watson statistic	2.46	2.17	2.18	1.55	2.25	2.22
Average of six subregressions	2.14					

*The forecast variable is the six-month excess return on long-term Treasury bonds. The forecast horizon is six months and the estimation period is from 1964 through 1993. The average Durbin-Watson statistic for the six subregressions is 2.14, indicating there is virtually no first-order serial correlation of the residuals in the model.

Sources:

Y, X_3, X_4: © *Stocks, Bonds, Bills, and Inflation 1996 Yearbook™*, Ibbotson Associates, Chicago (annually updates work by Roger G. Ibbotson and Rex A. Sinquefield). Used with permission. All rights reserved.

X_1: Federal Reserve Board (long-term Treasury yield) and U.S. Department of Labor (consumer price index);

X_2: U.S. Department of Labor.

X_5: Standard & Poor's. Used with permission of Standard & Poor's, a division of the McGraw-Hill Companies.

We will not repeat the search for influence point for the bond model described here and the models presented in Chapters 6 and 7 because the removal of a single point, or series of

TABLE 5-3

Post Regression Tests for the Bond Model*

	Real Interest Rate	Lagged Inflation	Log 2-Year Return S&P 500	6-Month T-Bill Return	12-Month Change Oil and Gold Stocks
	X_1	X_2	X_3	X_4	X_5
X_1	1.00				
X_2	0.37	1.00			
X_3	0.36	−0.04	1.00		
X_4	0.12	−0.67	0.01	1.00	
X_5	−0.01	−0.05	0.27	0.04	1.00

Test for Multicollinearity

Regression	Multiple R	R-Squared
X_1 vs. X_2, X_3, X_4, X_5	0.75	0.56
X_2 vs. X_1, X_3, X_4, X_5	0.84	0.70
X_3 vs. X_1, X_2, X_4, X_5	0.59	0.35
X_4 vs. X_1, X_2, X_3, X_5	0.80	0.65
X_5 vs. X_1, X_2, X_3, X_4	0.38	0.15

*The correlation matrix for the five predictor variables used for the bond market model shows that none of the pairwise correlations exceeds 0.85, the critical level discussed in Chapter 3. In addition, none of the multiple Rs exceed the 0.85 level in the test for multicollinearity.

Sources:
X_1: Federal Reserve Board (long-term Treasury yield) and U.S. Department of Labor (Consumer Price Index);
X_2: U.S. Department of Labor.
X_3, X_4: © Stocks, Bonds, Bills, and Inflation 1996 Yearbook™, Ibbotson Associates, Chicago (annually updates work by Roger G. Ibbotson and Rex A. Sinquefield). Used with permission. All rights reserved.
X_5: Standard & Poor's. Used with permission of Standard & Poor's, a division of the McGraw-Hill Companies.

points, does not change the regression output meaningfully. That's because the models in this book are structured in such a way that the likelihood of finding influence points is low. But the graphical and statistical techniques described in Chapter 4 nevertheless can be useful, especially if a model has fewer observations and fewer predictor variables than the models presented in this book. We will thus leave the check for influence points as an exercise for those readers who would like to pursue it.

6

A LARGE VERSUS SMALL CAPITALIZATION RELATIVE PERFORMANCE MODEL

Many investors have observed that small-capitalization stocks outperform large-capitalization stocks over time. The data is reasonably compelling. Small stocks, roughly defined as U.S. stocks with capitalizations among the smallest quintile of New York Stock Exchange issues, have outperformed the S&P 500 by about 1.5 percentage points a year since 1926. That may not sound like much, but it adds up over time owing to the effect of compounding, the "eighth wonder of the world."

Investing in small-company stocks, however, is not for the faint of heart. Indeed, small stocks are seen as riskier than large stocks, since their returns have been more volatile than large stock returns. Another problem is that the added performance doesn't come consistently: There are many multiyear periods when large stocks outperformed small stocks, and vice versa.

My interest in modeling the relative performance of large- and small-capitalization stocks had its origins when I was managing a market timing equity fund in the mid-1980s. In general, the fund held more stocks when our forecast was bullish and fewer stocks when our forecast was bearish. There were two ways to adjust the fund's stock market exposure. The first was straightforward: When our forecast changed in favor of equities, we could purchase more stocks or add to existing positions. Likewise, when our forecast called for a reduction in stock market exposure, issues held could be sold in their entirety or trimmed.

The other approach was to maintain a fully invested stock portfolio at all times and sell stock index futures contracts to reduce equity exposure. The process went as follows: A fund with a market value of $100 would be fully invested in individual stocks. If our stock market forecast called for 70 percent exposure to stocks, then we would sell stock index futures contracts with a market value of $30. As a result, the fund would be long $100 in equities through the individual stocks and short $30 in equities via the futures contracts. The net exposure to stocks was $70 or 70 percent of the total value of the fund.

The use of futures had two major benefits. First, as indicated earlier, changes in fund exposure could be executed without disturbing the underlying portfolio of individual stocks. Not having to buy or sell stocks as the market forecast changed made life easier and reduced the fund's capital gains liabilities. Second, the cost of buying and selling futures contracts was sharply lower than the cost of trading individual stocks.

There was one problem with using short futures positions as a hedge against the long equity portfolio. Each futures contract was linked to a specific stock market index. If the underlying index outperformed the stocks in our portfolio, we would lose a little money on the hedge. We tried to minimize this so-called tracking error by choosing the futures contract that best matched our stock portfolio.

As is true today, S&P futures were extremely liquid at the time, making them very cheap to trade. But the S&P 500 was dominated by the biggest 100 stocks, making it a "large-cap" index. Since we selected equities from a wide range of stocks, both large and small, and equally weighted our positions—a $100 portfolio might have had 100 one-dollar positions—we chose the broad-based, equally weighted and less liquid Value Line index for hedging the stock portfolio.

At the time we were well aware that large- and small-capitalization stock returns were often at variance with each other. If we could have modeled their relative performance, that is, forecast which group was likely to outperform the other, then we could have enhanced our portfolio returns by selling short the index that was likely to underperform.[13]

Being able to forecast the relative performance of large- and small-capitalization stocks is potentially useful to almost any institutional equity investor. A portfolio manager who believes smaller stocks are likely to outperform might decide to avoid big stocks like General Motors, Merck, or IBM. But such information can be tremendously useful to the individual mutual fund investor as well. That's because growth stock funds tend to avoid the big names that dominate the S&P 500. As a result, when large stocks dominate small stocks in terms of performance, the large-cap index funds designed to match the performance of the S&P 500 tend to beat the average growth stock fund. Likewise, when small-caps prevail, growth stock funds tend to outperform the large-cap index funds.

In the three years from 1991 through 1993, for example, small-company stocks outperformed large-company stocks by 13.6 percentage points a year, according to Ibbotson Associates. In those years, aggressive growth fund performance exceeded the large-cap index funds by about 10 percentage points annually, according to Morningstar, the mutual fund advisory service. Meanwhile, in the next two years (1994–95), small-stock performance faded. Indeed small stocks underperformed their larger-cap brethren modestly, according to Ibbotson Associates. In those two years, aggressive growth funds underperformed the large-cap index funds by 4.3 percentage points annually, according to Morningstar. In sum, forecasting small- versus large-capitalization relative stock performance is potentially useful to virtually all equity investors. Here's the model.

THE FORECAST VARIABLE

In this model the forecast variable is the annual return on small stocks less the annual return on large stocks, as published by Ibbotson Associates. In symbols the forecast variable can be written as:

$$(Small_{12}/Small_0) - (Large_{12}/Large_0)$$

where $Small_{12}$ and $Small_0$ are values of the Ibbotson small-cap stock total return index 12 months after the current month and in the current month, respectively; and $Large_{12}$ and $Large_0$ are values of the Ibbotson large-cap (S&P 500) stock total return index for the same months. The use of an annual horizon rather than the six-month returns used in the previous two chapters eliminates a problem with small-stock returns: Historically they have exhibited strong seasonality. Dubbed "the January effect" in financial literature, small stocks tend to outperform large stocks in the first quarter of the year. Since every 12-month return contains the seasonally strong period, there's no need to make seasonal adjustments to the forecasts. Of course, month-by-month forecasts of small-stock relative performance might be improved by trying to take advantage of the seasonal pattern, but this model will not address such an adjustment.

THE PREDICTOR VARIABLES

Here are the predictor variables for modeling the annual performance of small stocks relative to large stocks.

Predictor Variable 1: The 12-Month Percent Change in the Consumer Price Index Small stocks are thought to be beneficiaries of inflation, perhaps because small companies find it relatively easier to pass along price increases in inflationary times. In addition, high rates of inflation often are associated with rising economic output, which may benefit small stocks. Higher rates of inflation typically are associated with positive small-stock returns relative to large stock returns. In symbols, this variable is written as:

$$(CPI_{-1} / CPI_{-13}) - 1$$

where CPI_{-1} and CPI_{-13} represent the level of the **Consumer Price Index** one and 13 months previous to the current month. Again, the convention is to start from the level of the Consumer Price Index from the month previous to the current month since this figure is not reported until the current month.

Predictor Variable 2: The 12-Month Change in the Consumer Price Index Lagged 12 Months In conjunction with the first predictor variable, the lagged CPI allows the model to "know" whether inflation is accelerating, decelerating, or stable. The lagged inflation variable is also positively associated with the relative performance of small stocks. In symbols this variable is written as:

$$(CPI_{-13} / CPI_{-25}) - 1$$

for the Consumer Price Index 13 and 25 months before the current month.

Predictor Variable 3: The Average Yield on 10-Year Treasury Issues This data series, also called the 10-year Treasury constant maturity rate, is published by the Federal Reserve. The yield for each month is an average of daily figures. This can be written as:

$$CM10_0,$$

indicating it is the Treasury yield described above in the current month. This variable works together with the next variable.

Predictor Variable 4: The Average Yield on One-Year Treasury Issues The one-year constant maturity rate is also published by the Federal Reserve. This yield, also a monthly average of daily figures, can be written as

$$CM1_0,$$

indicating it is the one-year Treasury constant maturity yield for the current month.

The coefficients of the two yield variables work so that a widening spread between the 1- and 10-year Treasuries (i.e., when the yield curve is said to be steepening), is generally associated with good relative performance by small-cap stocks. When the spread narrows (i.e., when the yield curve flattens), small stocks tend not to do as well as large stocks. This is consistent with the widely observed phenomenon that steep yield curves are associated with a strong economy and good small-stock performance. Flat yield curves, however, are associated with weak economic growth and poor small-stock performance.

Predictor Variable 5: The 12-Month Change in the Credit Spread As discussed in Chapter 3, the credit quality spread, the difference between the yields on Baa and Aaa corporate bonds, is an indicator of confidence in the economy. A narrow spread means that investors have confidence in the economy; a wide spread indicates a lack of investor confidence. When the spread narrows, small stocks tend to perform better than large stocks; a widening spread often signals poor relative small-stock performance. The change is calculated by subtracting the level of the credit spread lagged 12 months from the current level of the spread. The variable is written as:

$$(Baa_0 - Aaa_0) - (Baa_{-12} - Aaa_{-12})$$

where the first term is the Baa and Aaa yields in the current month and the second term is made up of the same yields 12 months previous to the current month.

Predictor Variable 6: The 12-Month Change in the Credit Spread, Lagged 12 Months The lagged measure of the change in the credit spread is written in symbols as:

TABLE 6–1

Regression Output for a Model Forecasting the Performance of Small-Capitalization versus Large-Capitalization Stocks*

Constant	−0.27					
Standard error of Y estimate	0.11					
R-squared	0.55					
Number of observations	288					
Durbin-Watson statistic	0.32					

	12-Month Change CPIU	12-Month Change CPIU Lag 1 Year	10-Year Treasury Yield	1-Year Treasury Yield	12-Month Change Credit Spread	12-Month Change Credit Spread Lag 1 Year
	X_1	X_2	X_3	X_4	X_5	X_6
X-coefficient	4.08	2.27	0.07	−0.08	−1.09	−1.12
Standard error of X-coefficient	0.38	0.38	0.01	0.01	0.18	0.19
T-statistic	10.62	5.95	8.01	−11.32	−6.11	−5.85
Adjusted t-statistic	3.07	1.72	2.31	−3.27	−1.76	−1.69

*The forecast variable is the one-year total return on small-cap stocks less the one-year total return on large-cap stocks. The horizon is 12 months. The estimation period is from 1970 through 1993.

Sources:

Y: © *Stocks, Bonds, Bills, and Inflation 1996 Yearbook™*, Ibbotson Associates, Chicago (annually updates work by Roger G. Ibbotson and Rex A. Sinquefield). Used with permission. All rights reserved.

X_1 and X_2: U.S. Department of Labor;

X_3 and X_4: Federal Reserve Board;

X_5 and X_6: Moody's Investors Service. Used with permission.

$$(Baa_{-12} - Aaa_{-12}) - (Baa_{-24} - Aaa_{-24})$$

and has the same interpretation as its unlagged counterpart.

REGRESSION OUTPUT AND ANALYSIS

The regression output for the small-cap stock model is shown in Table 6–1. The R-squared is 0.55, meaning the model explains 55 percent of the squared variation of the one-year relative performance of small stocks over large stocks. As in the previous models, the Durbin-Watson statistic is skewed by the use of overlapping data. The average Durbin-Watson statistic for the 12 subregressions is 2.15, close enough to 2.00 to conclude that there is no serial correlation between the adjacent error terms.

There is something troubling about the regression output for the model, however. For three of the six variables, the adjusted t-statistic is not greater than 2.00 or less than –2.00, the rule-of-thumb cutoff for statistical significance for t-statistics. There are too many forecast variables for the data set. Recall that the forecast horizon for the model is 12 months. Since the estimation period runs from 1970 through 1993, there are only 24 independent observations of the forecast variable. The number of X variables needs to be reduced.

We'll start by eliminating the variable labeled X_2, the lagged inflation variable. We're also going to try consolidating the specification of the variables that describe the yield curve, the 10-year and 1-year Treasury yields. Rather than including both yields, the 1-year yield will be subtracted from the 10-year yield; the difference, which can be written as

$$CM10_0 - CM1_0,$$

will serve as a measure of the yield curve. When this new consolidated variable takes on high values, the yield curve is steep, suggesting economic strength down the road. The yield curve variable should be positively related to relative performance of small stocks over large stocks. Finally, we'll remove the variable labeled X_6, the lagged version of the credit spread.

The regression output for the new model is shown in Table 6–2. The explanatory power using the new specifications, as measured by the R-squared, drops from 0.55 to 0.47. Arguably, however, the larger number of variables in the original specification inflated the R-squared measure, so it may be fair to say that the explanatory power for the two models is largely the same.

T A B L E   6–2

Regression Output for a New Specification of the Small-Stock versus Large-Stock Model*

Constant	0.66		
Standard error of Y estimate	0.12		
R-squared	0.47		
Number of observations	288		
Durbin-Watson statistic	0.26		

	12-Month Change CPIU	Yield Curve	12-Month Change Credit Spread
	X_1	X_2	X_3
X-coefficient	5.17	0.08	−0.06
Standard error of X-coefficient	0.35	0.01	0.02
T-statistic	14.99	10.71	−3.21
Adjusted t-statistic	4.33	3.09	−0.93

*By removing and consolidating the X variables, the model was streamlined without losing much of its explanatory power. The adjusted t-statistic for the third independent variable suggests that it is not adding much explanatory power to the model, however.

Sources:
Y: © Stocks, Bonds, Bills, and Inflation 1996 Yearbook™, Ibbotson Associates, Chicago (annually updates work by Roger G. Ibbotson and Rex A. Sinquefield). Used with permission. All rights reserved.
X_1: U.S. Department of Labor;
X_2: Federal Reserve Board;
X_3: Moody's Investors Service. Used with permission.

A problem remains, however. The credit spread variable, with an adjusted t-statistic of only −0.93, is not carrying its weight. Let's look at some other ways that the credit spread could be specified.

Recall that the credit spread was calculated by subtracting the Aaa corporate bond yield from the Baa bond yield. Since Aaa bonds are of higher quality, they yield less than the lower-quality Baa bonds. Thus the credit spread, as defined, is positive. The actual variable used in the model is the 12-month change in the credit spread, calculated, for example, by taking the December 1994 level of the credit spread and subtracting the December 1993 figure from it.

Rather than subtracting the Aaa yield from the Baa yield, we could choose to divide the Baa yield by the Aaa yield (or vice versa). We could also take the reciprocal of the spread, that is, start with 1 and divide it by the difference between the Baa and Aaa yields. As long as the denominator never takes on the value 0, the reciprocal can be calculated. Several versions of this variable appear in Figure 6–1.

If other mathematical functions are considered fair game, there's no limit to the number of ways the credit spread (or for that matter, virtually all variables) can be defined. The logarithm of the ratio between the Baa and Aaa yields could be used. It might be possible to capture the cyclical nature of the data by using trigonometric functions. An analyst can square or take the square root of a variable (cube, or cube root, or any power). There are statistical transformations that confine a variable between 0 and 1 (cumulative normal function, for example). One trigonometric transformation, the arctangent function, keeps the adjusted variable between –pi/2 and +pi/2, or between approximately –1.57 and +1.57. One reason for considering these "confining" variables is that they diminish the effect of a forecast variable when it takes on a wildly high or low value. (Recall in our discussion of least squares that a large penalty is placed on outliers: an observation with a one-unit error has a squared error of one; an observation with a three-unit error has a squared error of nine.) Of course, with all statistical modeling work, the analyst should have a good reason for using a mathematical function to transform an explanatory variable.

The issue of whether to perform variable transformations leads to a broader question about modeling financial markets (or any forecast variable, for that matter). Each variable has easily a dozen ways to configure it. Moreover, variables can be

FIGURE 6–1

Configuring the Credit Spread

As initially constructed, this variable had little impact on model forecasts. Four possible variations are plotted below. Note the subtle differences. Months are reversed on the last chart to maintain the order of the variable.

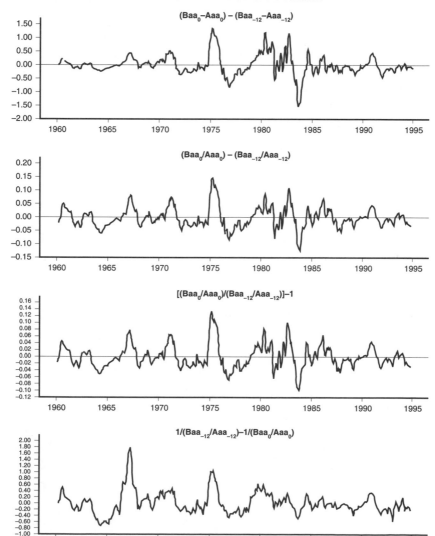

Source: Moody's Investors Service. Used with permission.

combined (as the credit spread) to form new variables. Finally, any model has at a minimum dozens of potential predictor variables. Now, for every variable we can consider its level, change, or change in change. A change can be computed over the last one, three, six or any number of months. Don't forget that lagged versions of a variable can be used as predictor variables. For example, if we are looking at the six-month change in long-term interest rates, we can use the current reading as well as readings from 6, 12 or any number of months previous to the current month. Clearly, all possible models cannot be tested. Over time, analysts develop a sense of how to screen out certain approaches as not likely to be fruitful. Experience also indicates that when basic strategies do not work, more exotic approaches are not likely to improve matters. Finally, if an unusual approach does seem to work, there is always the possibility that the apparent improvement will disappear when the model is tested by real-time forecasts.

As it turns out, using the 12-month change in the reciprocal of the credit spread does appear to add some explanatory power to the model, according to the regression output in Table 6–3. Note that the sign of the coefficient flips from negative to positive because taking the reciprocal of a variable reorders it in the opposite direction. That is, if a graph of the original variable goes downhill, then the reciprocal will go uphill. As with the previous models, the Durbin-Watson statistic is understated because of the use of overlapping data. The average D-W statistic for the 12 subregressions is 2.05, indicating virtually no correlation between adjacent error terms. Also shown in Table 6–3 is the correlation matrix for the predictor variables and the test results for multicollinearity among the predictor variables. None of the relationships exceeds the cutoff (or has a multiple R greater than 0.85) suggested in Chapter 3.

The credit spread variable remains problematic. Although the new specification has lifted the R-squared for the model, its adjusted t-statistic, at 1.55, is still below the rule-of-thumb cutoff

TABLE 6-3

Regression Output for a Final Specification of the Small-Stock versus Large-Stock Model*

Constant	−0.37		
Standard error of Y estimate	0.11		
R-squared	0.50		
Number of observations	288		
Durbin-Watson statistic	0.29		

	12-Month Change CPIU	Yield Curve	12-Month Change Credit Spread
	X_1	X_2	X_3
X-coefficient	5.53	0.08	0.15
Standard error of X-coefficient	0.34	0.01	0.03
T-statistic	16.50	11.39	5.35
Adjusted t-statistic	4.76	3.29	1.55

Correlation Matrix of Predictor Variables

	X_1	X_2	X_3
X_1	1.00		
X_2	−0.64	1.00	
X_3	−0.53	0.23	1.00

Test for Multicollinearity

	Multiple R	R-Squared
X_1 vs. X_2 and X_3	0.75	0.56
X_2 vs. X_1 and X_3	0.65	0.42
X_3 vs. X_1 and X_2	0.55	0.30

*In this version, the credit spread was calculated by taking the reciprocal of the difference between the Baa and Aaa corporate bond yields. Although the adjusted t-statistic for the credit spread variable has improved, it is still well below the rule-of-thumb cutoff of 2.00 for t-statistics. Whether to include it is a judgment call.

Sources:

Y: © Stocks, Bonds, Bills, and Inflation 1996 Yearbook™, Ibbotson Associates, Chicago (annually updates work by Roger G. Ibbotson and Rex A. Sinquefield). Used with permission. All rights reserved.

X_1: U.S. Department of Labor;

X_2: Federal Reserve Board;

X_3: Moody's Investors Services. Used with permission.

of 2.00. For now, the variable will be included in the model. As further research progresses, perhaps the model can be improved by adjusting the specification of the variable or by replacing it with an altogether new variable.

One possible improvement to the small-cap/large-cap model would be to include a variable based on the exchange rate of the U.S. dollar. The Federal Reserve, for example, publishes a dollar index series based on a basket of foreign currencies. The idea is that a rising dollar hurts the relative performance of large-capitalization stocks. That's because large stocks tend to have substantial operations overseas. A rising dollar diminishes the value of foreign profits translated back into the home currency. Unfortunately, attempts to incorporate the dollar into the small-stock/large-stock model were unsuccessful. There is a meaningful correlation between the dollar and the forecast variable. However, the other three variables seem to capture most of the information the dollar has to offer, since adding the dollar as a predictor variable did not improve the model.

A forward-looking analyst might well persist in trying to include a variable based on the dollar in a small-stock/large-stock model because large-capitalization companies have become increasingly global over the past several years. As a result, non–dollar denominated profits were more important in the second half of the estimation period than they were in first half. So it is possible that the model understates the predictive value of a dollar-based variable.

One way to try to flush out evidence that the dollar exchange rate has become an increasingly important explanatory variable is to reweight the observations in favor of the more recent part of the estimation period. For example, over the years from 1970 through 1993, the observations from 1971 might be duplicated once, from 1972, twice, and so on through 1994. As result of this reconfiguration of the data set, observations from 1993 will outnumber the 1970 observations by a factor of 24 and they will be twice as numerous as the observations from 1981.

Using the 12-month percent change in the Federal Reserve Board dollar index, which dates back to 1967, the reweighting scheme does lift the greenback's contribution to forecasting small-cap/large-cap relative price performance. The result offers some empirical confirmation of the dollar-is-more-important-now hypothesis. The problem, of course, is that the choice of a reweighting scheme is arbitrary. Care has to be taken not to "mine the data," that is, create what appears to be an excellent model for the years from 1970 through 1993, but produces poor forecasts from 1994 and beyond.

7

A CANADIAN
DOLLAR MODEL

My interest in the Canadian dollar began when I was managing a Canadian mutual fund. One of the first things I learned about Canadian investors is that they loved to hate their home currency and generally prefer the U.S. dollar as a storehouse of value. Two issues were weighing on the Canadian dollar in the mid-1990s: First, the province of Quebec always seemed to be on the verge of secession. Second, Canada's budget deficit was running at 5 percent to 6 percent of gross domestic product versus about 2 percent for the United States.

While maintaining U.S. dollar exposure will allow Canadian investors to book currency gains when the Canadian dollar is declining against the U.S. dollar, a rally or sustained rise in the Canadian dollar relative to its U.S. counterpart can create losses, a situation that promotes interest in forecasting the $Canada/$U.S. exchange rate. An accurate forecast solidly in favor of the $Canada might save Canadian investors from currency losses. Meanwhile, U.S. investors could benefit from such a forecast by shifting a portion of their investment portfolios into

Canadian-denominated stocks and bonds, or they could even park excess cash in Canadian Treasury bills.

THE FORECAST VARIABLE

The forecast variable for the Canadian dollar exchange rate will be the 12-month percent change in the number of U.S. dollars per Canadian dollar, as published by the Federal Reserve Board. In symbols we can write it as:

$$\$C_{12} / \$C_0 - 1$$

where $\$C_{12}$ and $\$C_0$ are exchange rates for the Canadian dollar denominated in U.S. dollars 12 months subsequent to the current month and the current month, respectively. Since these figures are monthly averages of daily rates, we'll be on guard that the regression output may overstate the explanatory power of the model. That's because monthly averages dampen some of the noise caused by daily price fluctuations. This noise in the forecast variable will be hidden from the model, so it is likely that the R-squared will be overstated. The good news is that, since the forecast horizon is 12 months, the forecast variable based on monthly averages is highly correlated (typical correlation: about 0.97) with the same variable based on daily data.

A second limitation to this model is the size of the data set. Exchange rates did not float freely until the early 1970s; given the lags in the predictor variables to be proposed below, the data set begins in 1975. As with the other models proposed in this book, the data ends in 1993, providing only 19 independent annual observations.

THE PREDICTOR VARIABLES

Here are the predictor variables for the Canadian dollar model.

Predictor Variable 1: Canadian/U.S. Relative Inflation   *Relative inflation* is defined as the ratio between the Canadian and U.S.

Consumer Price Indexes. The variable is lagged one month to account for the fact that the figure for one month is reported in the following month. The variable is written in symbols as

$$CPIcan_{-1} / CPIus_{-1},$$

indicating that it is ratio of the level of the Canadian CPI one month previous to the current month divided by the comparable figure for the United States.

This variable is based on the notion of *purchasing power parity*, a widely used approach to studying exchange rates that we will discuss briefly.

To save on some arithmetic, suppose the U.S. dollar/Canadian dollar exchange rate (hereafter, the $C exchange rate) is at parity: one U.S. dollar equals one Canadian dollar. If a Big Mac costs $2 U.S. in Niagara Falls, NY, but only $1.50 Canadian across the Niagara River in Canada, then an enterprising soul could theoretically buy burgers in Canada for $1.50 Canadian, run across the Rainbow Bridge to the U.S. side of the border, and sell them for $2 U.S. Since $1 U.S. equals $1 Canadian, then the arbitrageur could pocket 50¢ per burger.

Presumably, a free and frictionless market should keep prices in line, but there are a number of potential impediments to perfect purchasing power parity. For example, it may be that our entrepreneur must buy Canadian dollars for $1.05 U.S. and sell them for $0.95 U.S., which would cut into his profit margin. Customs officials at the border might charge a duty on each burger that comes into the United States, further cutting into the gross profit margin. Perhaps the special sauce on Canadian burgers is slightly different than the sauce on their U.S. counterparts, according to national tastes. U.S. customers, as a result, might not pay the full $2 for the Canadian imports.

Despite the potential imperfections, it makes sense that cross-border prices should be roughly equal, upholding the "law of one price." It follows that if inflation in Canada is running at a 10 percent annual pace, and U.S. inflation is only 5 percent, then the Canadian dollar should depreciate about 5 percent a year against the greenback in order to maintain purchasing power parity.

Hence the use of the Canadian CPI relative to the U.S. CPI. A rise (decline) in Canadian inflation relative to U.S. inflation should be accompanied by a decline (rise) in the $C exchange rate.

Predictor Variable 2: The 24-Month Percent Change in Oil Stock Prices, Lagged 24 Months This variable, which takes into consideration that natural resources constitute a larger share of Canadian output than U.S. output, can be written in symbols as

$$OIL_{-24}/OIL_{-48} - 1,$$

indicating that it is the ratio of Standard & Poor's oil stock index 24 months previous to the current month to the same index 48 months previous to the current month, less one to turn the figure into a percent change in decimal form.

Using oil stock prices as a proxy for natural resource prices, we expect a rise in this variable to be accompanied by an increase in the number of U.S. dollars going to Canada to pay for U.S. purchases of Canadian natural resources. Now assume that Canada recycles its U.S. dollars by buying some composite of U.S. goods and services, the price, and quantity of which has not changed. Canada will find itself with a growing and unneeded supply of U.S. dollars, causing the Canadian dollar to rise relative to the U.S. dollar. The two-year lag reflects the notion that the mechanism is a slow-moving one.

Predictor Variable 3: The 24-Month Percent Change in the $C Exchange Rate, Lagged 24 Months This is a lagged trend variable that tries to take advantage of the fact that currency exchange rate changes, including the $C exchange rate, are correlated with past rate changes. It can be written in symbols as:

$$\$C_{-24}/\$C_{-48}$$

indicating that it is the value of the Canadian dollar, denominated in U.S. dollars 24 months previous to the current month divided by the same figure 48 months previous to the current month. Both the numerator and denominator are monthly averages of daily rates.

Predictor Variable 4: The Canadian Treasury Bill Rate, Lagged 24 Months This is a lagged measure of the Canadian short-term interest rates. Written in symbols as

$$TBcan_{-24}$$

it is the rate 24 months previous to the current month. This variable, also configured as a monthly average of daily rates, serves as proxy for the strength of the Canadian economy. Alternatively, it can be seen as a proxy for the level of inflation in the Canadian economy.[14]

REGRESSION OUTPUT AND ANALYSIS

Table 7–1 shows the regression output of the $C exchange rate model. The forecast horizon is 12 months and the estimation period is the 19 years from 1975 through 1993. The R-squared is 0.59, meaning that 59 percent of the squared variation of the 12-month change in $C exchange rate is explained by the model. All of the t-statistics, adjusted for the overlapping data, are significant.

There are some surprises in the signs of the X-coefficients. A negative sign was expected for the relative inflation (X_1) variable, but the empirical result was just the opposite. One explanation is that the relative inflation variable, at least in the short term, is a proxy for relative economic strength, which favors the currency of the faster growing country. Since the other three variables have two-year lags, the signs of the coefficients, in retrospect, might have been thought to be difficult to guess. The

TABLE 7–1

Regression Output for the $Canadian/$U.S. Exchange Rate Model*

Constant	0.72
Standard error of Y estimate	0.03
R-squared	0.59
Number of observations	228
Durbin-Watson statistic	0.35

	Relative Canada/U.S. CPI	2-Year Change Oil Stocks Lag 2 Years	2-Year Change $C/$US Rate Lag 2 Years	Canadian T-Bill Rate Lag 2 Years
	X_1	X_2	X_3	X_4
X-coefficient	0.60	0.07	−0.34	−0.01
Standard error of X-coefficient	0.05	0.01	0.03	0.00
T-statistic	11.73	9.94	−11.06	−12.21
Adjusted t-statistic	3.39	2.87	−3.19	−3.52

	Jan.	Feb.	Mar.	Apr.	May	June
Durbin-Watson statistics	2.56	2.77	2.17	2.59	2.23	2.35
	Jul	Aug	Sep	Oct	Nov	Dec
	2.49	2.26	2.18	2.60	2.75	2.48
Average of 12 subregressions	2.45					

*The forecast variable is the one-year percent change in the Canadian dollar priced in U.S. dollars. The forecast horizon is 12 months and the estimation period is from 1975 through 1993.

Sources:
Y: Federal Reserve Board;
X_1: Bank of Canada (Canadian CPI) and the U.S. Department of Labor (U.S. CPI).
X_2: Standard & Poor's. Used with permission of Standard & Poor's, a division of the McGraw-Hill Companies.
X_3: Federal Reserve Board;
X_4: Bank of Canada.

oil stock price variable, however, does have the postulated positive sign.

As with all of the models proposed in this book, the low Durbin-Watson statistic incorrectly implies that the error terms are positively autocorrelated, due to the use of overlapping data. The average Durbin-Watson statistic for the 12 subregressions, shown at the bottom of Table 7–1, is 2.45. According to the table supplied by Durbin and Watson, the average falls in the lower end of the "indeterminate" range between 2.15 and 3.14. Had the average Durbin-Watson statistic exceeded 3.14, that would have constituted strong evidence of negative serial correlation of the error terms. Had the average fallen between 1.85 and 2.15, then the conclusion would have been that no serial correlation was present. Once again, the interpretation of the Durbin-Watson statistic may be clouded by the inclusion of a lagged form of the forecast variable as a predictor variable in the model.

In this case an AR(12) term was added to the model in an attempt to take advantage of the possibility that negative serial correlation of every 12th error term is present. (Equivalently, we could have added an AR(1) term to each of the 12 subregressions.) The new regression (not shown) lifted the R-squared of the model only marginally from 0.59 to 0.61, and the t-statistic for the AR term was not significant. The inclusion of an autoregressive term does not appear to improve the model, so it will remain as it was initially proposed.

The pairwise correlation matrix for the four predictor variables is shown in Table 7–2. None of the correlations is meaningfully high. Moreover, none of the multiple Rs for the multicollinearity test (also shown in Table 7–2) come close to 0.85, indicating that there is no problem with multicollinearity.

T A B L E 7–2

Pairwise Correlation Matrix for Four Predictor Variables*

	Relative Canada/U.S. CPI	2-Year Change Oil Stocks Lag 2 Years	2-Year Change $C/$US Rate Lag 2 Years	Canadian T-Bill Rate Lag 2 Years
	X_1	X_2	X_3	X_4
X_1	1.000			
X_2	0.228	1.000		
X_3	0.266	0.133	1.000	
X_4	0.460	0.231	−0.091	1.000

Test for Multicollinearity

Regression	Multiple R	R-Squared
X_1 vs. X_2, X_3, and X_4	0.56	0.31
X_2 vs. X_1, X_3, and X_4	0.29	0.09
X_3 vs. X_1, X_2, and X_4	0.37	0.14
X_4 vs. X_1, X_2, and X_3	0.53	0.28

*Variables used for the regression reported in Table 7–1. Also shown are the multiple R and R-squared measures for each of four regressions: X_1 vs. X_2, X_3, and X_4; X_2 vs. X_1, X_3, and X_4; etc. None of the multiple Rs exceed 0.85, the critical level cited in Chapter 3.

Sources:
X_1: Bank of Canada (Canadian CPI) and the U.S. Department of Labor (U.S. CPI).
X_2: Standard & Poor's. Used with permission of Standard & Poor's, a division of the McGraw-Hill Companies.
X_3: Federal Reserve Board.
X_4: Bank of Canada.

III

HOW TO USE MARKET TIMING FORECASTS

8

EXPLORING THE POTENTIAL FOR GAINS FROM MARKET TIMING

Any investor about to make investment decisions based on the output of a forecasting process probably would like to know the chances of beating the alternative of investing passively. The investor might be planning to self-manage a strategy or considering hiring an investment advisor who claims to be able to add value by methodically varying exposure to an asset class like common stocks. The process might be strictly quantitatively based, like the models proposed in this book, or based on a mixture of judgments, both quantitative and qualitative, of a wide array of information including asset valuations, the state of the economy, monetary and fiscal policy, the foreign sector, technical analysis and investor sentiment.

In this chapter we will attempt to make a first approximation of potential gains from market timing. The approach will use idealized returns and forecasts, so care has to be taken in assuming the results can be transferred directly to the real world. Deviations from the idealized environment will be discussed at length in the next chapter.

SETTING UP A HYPOTHETICAL INVESTMENT ENVIRONMENT

As a first step we're going to create a hypothetical series of monthly stock market returns. The returns will be determined by a random number generator and be normally distributed. The compound annual return for the series will be 12 percent, approximately equal to the long-term average annual return on common stocks. The annualized standard deviation of the returns will be 16 percent, considerably lower than the volatility of stocks since the 1920s, but in line with the post–World War II experience. A companion series of constant monthly Treasury bill returns also will be created with a compound annual return of 5 percent. Thus, the average excess return on stocks over the risk-free return has been set at 7 percent, approximately equal to the long-term average.

The next step is to create hypothetical stock market forecasts with varying degrees of explanatory power. Five sets of forecasts were created: one with a 10 percent correlation with the next month's (simulated) stock return, and one with a 20 percent, a 30 percent, a 40 percent, and a 50 percent correlation. A sixth forecast series was created with no explanatory power, that is, a series with a 0 percent correlation with the simulated stock returns.

Each of the six raw forecast series was regressed against the excess stock return series. Based on the regression output, adjusted excess return forecasts were created that take into consideration the explanatory power of each forecast series. That is, for each raw forecast series, the constant from the regression was added to the product of the X-coefficient of the regression and the raw forecast.

The adjusted excess return forecasts were transformed into series that access the probability that stocks will outperform Treasury bills. This was done by creating what are called Z-scores by dividing the adjusted excess return forecasts by the standard error of each regression. The Z-scores were transformed into probabilities using a statistical software program capable of

TABLE 8–1

Regression-Based Forecasts Divided by the Standard Error of the Regression*

Z-Score	Probability	Z-Score	Probability
−3.00	0.1%	0.10	54.0%
−2.00	2.3	0.20	57.9
−1.80	3.6	0.30	61.8
−1.60	5.5	0.40	65.5
−1.40	8.1	0.50	69.1
−1.20	11.5	0.60	72.6
−1.00	15.9	0.70	75.8
−0.90	18.4	0.80	78.8
−0.80	21.2	0.90	81.6
−0.70	24.2	1.00	84.1
−0.60	27.4	1.20	88.5
−0.50	30.9	1.40	91.9
−0.40	34.5	1.60	94.5
−0.30	38.2	1.80	96.4
−0.20	42.1	2.00	97.7
−0.10	46.0	3.00	99.9
0.00	50.0		

*The resultant Z-scores can be transformed into probabilities by using a statistical software package.

calculating normal distribution statistics. Selected Z-scores and their associated probabilities are shown in Table 8–1. The overall process described above is summarized in Table 8–2.

Let's take a moment to review the information in Table 8–2. The R-squared in the regression output is 0.09. Since there is only one X-variable in the regression, the raw forecast series, the square root of the R-squared ($\sqrt{0.09} = 0.30$) is the correlation between the raw forecast and the excess stock returns. Notice that the X-coefficient of the regression is 0.30, the same as the correlation. What this means is that the raw forecasts are "shrunk" at a rate proportional to the explanatory power of the model. A 10 percent raw forecast, excluding the effect of the constant, is

TABLE 8–2

Simulating Market Timing Potential*

Stock Return	T-Bill Return	Excess Stock Return	Raw Forecast Correlation =.30	Adjusted Forecast	Z-Score	Probability That Stocks Outperform T-Bills
0.012	0.004	0.008	0.040	0.015	0.330	62.9%
−0.031	0.004	−0.035	−0.066	−0.017	−0.394	34.7%
−0.002	0.004	−0.007	−0.037	−0.009	−0.196	42.2%
0.044	0.004	0.040	0.123	0.039	0.895	81.5%
0.013	0.004	0.009	0.055	0.019	0.428	66.6%
0.094	0.004	0.090	0.030	0.011	0.259	60.2%
0.073	0.004	0.069	0.052	0.018	0.413	66.0%
−0.014	0.004	−0.018	−0.042	−0.010	−0.231	40.9%
0.019	0.004	0.015	0.010	0.006	0.126	55.0%
0.007	0.004	0.003	0.050	0.018	0.399	65.5%
–	–	–	–	–	–	–
–	–	–	–	–	–	–
–	–	–	–	–	–	–
−0.036	0.004	−0.040	−0.019	−0.003	−0.071	47.2%
−0.009	0.004	−0.013	0.024	0.010	0.219	58.7%
−0.039	0.004	−0.043	−0.023	−0.005	-0.104	45.8%

Constant	0.002
Standard error of Y estimate	0.044
R-squared	0.090
Number of observations	6000
X-coefficient	0.300
Standard error of X-coefficient	0.012
T-statistic	24.385

*Normally distributed stock returns were created with a 12 percent compound annual return and a 16 percent annualized standard deviation. Constant T-bill returns were created with a 5 percent compound annual return. The excess stock returns equal the difference between the stock and T-bill returns, making the annualized excess return 7 percent. The raw forecasts have a 30 percent correlation with the stock returns.

Output for the regression of the excess stock returns against the raw forecasts is shown at the bottom of this table. The adjusted forecasts equal the regression constant plus the product of the X-coefficient and the X-variable, the raw forecasts. The Z-score is the ratio of the adjusted forecast and the standard error of Y-estimate. The Z-scores are transformed into probabilities using a statistical software package or are approximated using a standardized normal distribution table found in the back of virtually all statistical textbooks.

reduced to 3 percent. Likewise, a –10 percent forecast is "reduced" to –3 percent. This result is exactly in line with what we would like. If a model with low explanatory power generates a very bullish raw forecast, the adjusted forecast is reined in. The same raw forecast from a more powerful model, meanwhile, would be taken more seriously.[15]

Estimating the Potential to Add Value: Strategy 1

Now let's consider the potential value added from using the simulated forecasts. By construction, a buy-and-hold strategy will earn the passive investor a 12 percent compound annual return with an annualized standard deviation of 16 percent. In order to estimate the value of an active investment program driven by model forecasts, decision rules for investing need to be established. If the probability is 80 percent that stocks are going to outperform Treasury bills, how much is invested in stocks and how much in Treasury bills? Can funds be borrowed to leverage up the investment? If the probability that stocks outperform Treasury bills falls to a bearish 10 percent, could stocks be sold short in order to profit from a stock market decline?

The first strategy we'll consider is to be 100 percent long in stocks if the probability that stocks outperform Treasury bills exceeds 50 percent; otherwise the portfolio will be 100 percent invested in Treasury bills. The results of this strategy are shown in Table 8–3.

One notable outcome of this strategy is that use of the forecasts that don't add information (where the forecast correlation is 0 percent) generates exactly the same return as the buy-and-hold strategy. When there is no information about excess stock returns, the best forecast is a constantly positive one, since the simulated excess stock returns, on average, are greater than zero. As a result, the zero-correlation forecasts always call for the probability that stocks outperform Treasury bills be greater than 50 percent. Under the rules of Strategy 1, the zero-correlation

TABLE 8–3

Simulating Market Timing Potential Using Strategy 1*

		Compound Annual Return	Annualized Standard Deviation	Annual Turnover	Average Exposure to Stocks
Buy and hold		12.0%	16.0%	0%	100%
Forecast correlation:	0%	12.0	16.0	0	100
Forecast correlation:	10	12.0	15.3	175	92
Forecast correlation:	20	14.0	13.8	436	76
Forecast correlation:	30	16.2	13.0	519	68
Forecast correlation:	40	18.7	12.5	544	64
Forecast correlation:	50	21.4	12.1	558	61

*In this simulation, the investor was hypothetically fully invested in stocks if the probability that stocks outperform Treasury bills was greater than 50 percent; otherwise the investor was fully invested in Treasury bills.

portfolio is thus fully invested at all times, making it the equivalent of the buy-and-hold portfolio.

In this simulation, the 10 percent correlation forecasts do not improve the compound annual return, but they do reduce the standard deviation a bit. As the forecast correlations rise from 20 percent to 50 percent, however, the compound annual returns advance smartly as the standard deviation goes down. As forecasts incorporate more explanatory power, the investor tends to be in stocks more when stocks are rising and in Treasury bills more when stocks are declining. This means the investor is increasingly participating in the upside volatility and decreasingly participating in the downside volatility, the twin results being a higher rate of return and a lower overall volatility.

Now we'll consider the turnover data briefly. First let "100 percent annual turnover" mean that an investment portfolio is replaced completely once over the course of a year. The investor could shift the composition of one-fourth of the portfolio four times or replace the whole portfolio once during the year, for example.

The turnover information is included because there are costs involved in buying and selling stocks and Treasury bills, depending on the market value of the portfolio involved. Arguably, an individual investor with $100,000 in a no-load mutual fund family could move from stocks to a money market fund at no cost. A large pension plan, however, with billions of dollars to move around would incur costs that would reduce the potential gains from using forecasts to actively manage an investment portfolio. The turnover data is included to give an indication of the amount of trading involved in executing a strategy.

Estimating the Potential to Add Value: Strategy 2

In the next strategy, the portfolio's exposure to stocks will be varied according to the probability that stocks are going to outperform Treasury bills. Indeed, the percentage exposure to stocks will be set equal to the probability that stocks are going to outperform Treasury bills. The remainder of the portfolio will be invested in Treasury bills. That is, if the probability that stocks outperform bills, expressed in percentage terms, is P, then the exposure to stocks will equal P and the exposure to Treasury bills will equal $100-P$.

This second strategy has some intuitive appeal. As the forecast becomes increasingly bullish, more money is put into stocks. Likewise, bearish forecasts result in low exposures to stocks. Compare this with the first strategy that put 100 percent of a portfolio in stocks when the probability P was either 51 percent or 99 percent. The results of this strategy are shown in Table 8–4.

The simulated returns are interesting for the second strategy because they allow both proponents and opponents of market timing to misrepresent the results. An investment advisor arguing against market timing might claim that market timers don't add value because even the market timer whose forecasts actually have a 30 percent correlation with the next month's stock market return underperforms a buy-and-hold strategy.

T A B L E   8–4

Simulating Market Timing Potential Using Strategy 2*

		Compound Annual Return	Annualized Standard Deviation	Annual Turnover	Average Exposure to Stocks
Buy and hold		12.0%	16.0%	0%	100%
Forecast correlation:	0%	9.2	8.9	7	56
Forecast correlation:	10	9.4	8.9	54	56
Forecast correlation:	20	10.1	9.0	107	56
Forecast correlation:	30	11.3	9.2	161	56
Forecast correlation:	40	13.0	9.4	215	56
Forecast correlation:	50	15.1	9.7	271	56

*In this simulation the investor's hypothetical percentage investment in stocks is equal to the probability that stocks outperform Treasury bills. The remainder of the portfolio is allocated to Treasury bills.

Meanwhile, the market timer who actually has no forecast information might claim to have earned 77 percent of the return of stocks (9.2%/12.0%) but only exposed the investor to 56 percent (8.9%/16.0%) of the risk, thus earning a superior risk-adjusted return.

There is a problem with both arguments. The market timer following this strategy with 30 percent correlation forecasts will never be 100 percent invested in stocks. Thus, it will difficult, even with forecasts that contain information, to outperform a generally rising market. The argument of the advisor without information can be reduced to the absurd by pointing out that an investor who maintains a 100 percent investment in Treasury bills will earn 42 percent (5.0%/12.0%) of the return and take on none of the risk, since Treasury bill returns are known with certainty at the time of purchase. When an investor looks at the excess return earned (the return on investment less the Treasury bill return) relative to the risk taken on, there's not much to distinguish the advisor with no information who maintains a steadily low exposure to stocks from the buy-and-hold investor who is fully invested. In this strategy the zero-correlation forecasts produce about 60 percent ((9.0%–5.0%)/(12.0%–5.0%)) of the excess return and take on 56 percent (8.9%/16.0%) of the risk.[16]

One conclusion to draw here is that the results of a strategy using forecasts should be compared to the hypothetical execution of the same strategy without the benefit of any information, that is, the same strategy using the zero-correlation forecasts. Note that both strategies showed marked improvement in returns relative to the zero-correlation baseline as the forecast correlations rose from 10 percent to 50 percent.

Estimating the Potential to Add Value: Strategy 3 and Summary

The last strategy to be considered in this chapter will make more efficient use of the information in the forecasts. The percentage stock exposure will equal twice the probability P less 100 percent. The percentage investment in Treasury bills will equal 200 percent less twice the probability P. This will allow stock exposure to vary from –100 percent to +100 percent. An allocation schedule for this strategy is shown in Table 8–5.

There is an accounting issue to deal with when a negative (i.e., short) stock position is established. Somebody earns interest income on the short sale proceeds and that somebody is the short seller. So if an investor who is 100 percent invested in Treasury bills enters into a 20 percent short stock position, overall exposure to Treasury bills will rise to 120 percent (100 percent from the original investment plus 20 percent more from the short sale proceeds). The convention used here is reasonably close to actually establishing a short position in the market using stock index futures.

The results of the third strategy simulation, shown in Table 8–6, are striking because the excess returns relative to the standard deviations are exceedingly high. For example, using the 30 percent correlation forecasts, the excess return (10.0% – 5.0% =

T A B L E   8–5

Allocation Schedule for Strategy 3*

Probability That Stocks Outperform Treasury Bills	Percent Portfolio Invested in Stocks	Percent Portfolio Invested in Treasury Bills
0%	−100%	200%
10	−80	180
20	−60	160
30	−40	140
40	−20	120
50	0	100
60	20	80
70	40	60
80	60	40
90	80	20
100	100	0

*The percent of the portfolio invested in stocks equals twice the probability P that stocks will outperform Treasury bills less 100 percent ($2P - 100$). The percent of the portfolio invested in Treasury bills equals $200 - 2P$. Proceeds of short sales are invested in Treasury bills, allowing the funds invested in Treasury bills to exceed 100 percent when a short position in stocks is established.

5.0%) divided by the standard deviation (4.4%) equals 1.14. In the second strategy this efficiency ratio for the 30 percent correlation forecasts was ($11.3\% - 5.0\% = 6.3\%$)/$9.2\% = 0.68$. In the first strategy the comparable figure was ($16.2\% - 5.0\% = 11.2\%$)/13.0% = 0.86. Apparently, the most efficient strategy is the third one, followed by the first one, and then the second. These results are shown in Table 8–7.

Strategy 2 has the lowest efficiency ratio because it makes the worst use of the information in the forecasts. When the forecasts are bullish, this strategy gets increasingly invested in stocks. But the strategy maintains an investment in stocks when the forecasts are bearish, that is, when stocks are likely to underperform Treasury bills. Strategy 1, meanwhile, avoids stocks

TABLE 8–6

Strategy 3*

		Compound Annual Return	Annualized Standard Deviation	Annual Turnover	Average Exposure to Stocks
Buy and hold		12.0%	16.0%	0%	100%
Forecast correlation:	0%	5.9	1.8	14	11
Forecast correlation:	10	6.3	2.2	107	12
Forecast correlation:	20	7.7	3.2	214	16
Forecast correlation:	30	10.0	4.4	322	21
Forecast correlation:	40	13.3	5.8	431	27
Forecast correlation:	50	17.7	7.1	541	34

*In this simulation the investor's hypothetical percentage investment in stocks is equal to $2P - 100$, where P equals the probability that stocks outperform Treasury bills. The investment in Treasury bills equals $200 - 2P$. For this strategy the average exposure to stocks was calculated as the average of the absolute values of the stock exposures—the sign for short positions was flipped from negative to positive.

altogether when forecasts are bearish. Strategy 3 goes one step further by taking advantage of the likelihood that stocks are going to underperform Treasury bills by shorting the stock market when the forecasts are bearish. Hence Strategy 3 has the highest efficiency ratio. For investors unable to short the stock market, Strategy 2 can be improved by maintaining 100 percent exposure to Treasury bills whenever the probability that stocks are going to outperform bills falls below 50 percent. This approach will save the investor from being exposed to stocks when they are likely to underperform Treasury bills.

T A B L E 8–7

Efficiency Ratios for Three Strategies*

Strategy Number	Excess Return	Standard Deviation	Efficiency Ratio
1	11.2%	13.0%	0.86
2	6.3	9.2	0.68
3	5.0	4.4	1.14
Buy-and-hold	7.0	16.0	0.44

Differences in Exposure to Stocks for the Three Strategies

	Strategy 1	Strategy 2	Strategy 3
Prob. = 0.00	0%	0%	−100%
Prob. = 0.10	0	10	−80
Prob. = 0.20	0	20	−60
Prob. = 0.30	0	30	−40
Prob. = 0.40	0	40	−20
Prob. = 0.50	0	50	0
Prob. = 0.60	100	60	20
Prob. = 0.70	100	70	40
Prob. = 0.80	100	80	60
Prob. = 0.90	100	90	80
Prob. = 1.00	100	100	100

*Using 30 percent correlation forecasts and the passive buy-and-hold alternative.

9

SIMULATING PERFORMANCE OF MARKET TIMING MODELS

In this chapter we will try to estimate potential gains from using the models introduced in Section 2. That is, we'll compare the hypothetical use of the model forecasts against forecasts that provide no information (zero-correlation forecasts). But first we'll consider three factors that can reduce gains from market timing: chance, the data gathering process, and the possibility of a major unforseen shift in the economy.

APPARENT DEVIATIONS IN THE DISTRIBUTION OF RETURNS

Short-term variations in return volatility and forecast correlations can cause actual outcomes from using market timing models to differ from the expected gains described in Chapter 8. Recall that the results posted in the last chapter were based on 6,000 monthly returns—500 years of data—that were normally distributed and had a constant standard deviation. The forecast correlations, meanwhile, were also measured over the 500-year

T A B L E   9-1

How Short-Term Estimates of Volatility Can Vary from Time to Time*

	Number of Periods in Group	Range of Estimated Standard Deviations
Lowest 10% of two-year periods	25	9.4%–12.7%
Next 20% of two-year periods	50	12.7%–14.2%
Middle 40% of two-year periods	100	14.2%–16.6%
Next 20% of two-year periods	50	16.7%–18.4%
Highest 10% of two-year periods	25	18.5%–22.7%

*The 500 years of hypothetical stock returns were divided into 250 two-year periods, each with 24 monthly observations. The standard deviation for each two-year period was estimated. Summary statistics are shown in the table.

period. Although summary statistics such as standard deviations and correlations are known for the 500-year period, estimates of those figures will vary over different time frames.

The first short-term variation to consider is the standard deviation. Recall that the hypothetical stock return series had an annualized standard deviation of 16 percent. If a higher level of volatility had been chosen, then the potential gains from market timing would have been higher. A lower level of volatility would have resulted in lower potential gains. That's because when asset returns are more volatile, there is more variance to be explained for each level of forecast correlation. Short-term variations in volatility, compared to the expected level of volatility, as a result, can cause short-term gains from market timing to differ from expected gains from market timing.

This idea is shown in Table 9–1, in which the 500 years of stock returns were divided into 250 two-year series, each with 24 monthly returns. The annualized standard deviation was estimated for each of the 250 subgroups. The results show that in 10 percent of the two-year periods, the estimated standard deviation fell below 12.7 percent, compared to the 16 percent standard deviation for the overall series. The standard deviation

T A B L E   9-2

How Short-Term Estimates of Correlation Can Vary from Time to Time*

	Number of Periods in Group	Range of Estimated Correlations
Lowest 10% of two-year periods	25	−0.35 to 0.05
Next 20% of two-year periods	50	0.05 to 0.21
Middle 40% of two-year periods	100	0.21 to 0.40
Next 20% of two-year periods	50	0.40 to 0.55
Highest 10% of two-year periods	25	0.55 to 0.78

*The 500 years of hypothetical stock returns and the 30 percent correlation forecasts were divided into 250 two-year periods, each with 24 monthly observations. The correlation between the stock returns and the 30 percent correlation forecasts was estimated for each two-year period. Summary statistics for the range of estimated correlations are shown in the table.

exceeded 18.5 percent in 10 percent of the two-year periods with the highest estimated standard deviations.

Wide ranges in the volatility of stock market returns have been a fact of life in recent years. In the two years ended 1988, the estimated standard deviation of S&P 500 returns was about 22 percent. In the two years ended 1993, meanwhile, the figure was only 7 percent. Assuming a market timer had a model with the same correlation in both periods, there was tremendous opportunity to add value in the late 1980s period but very little opportunity to add value in the early 1990s period.

Similarly, if a market model has a known correlation with future stock market returns, the measured correlation will fluctuate from time to time due to chance. In order to prepare Table 9–2 the 500 years of hypothetical stock market returns and the 30 percent correlation forecasts were divided into 250 two-year periods, each with 24 monthly observations. Here, the results show a range of correlations from −0.35 to 0.05 for the 10 percent of the two-year periods with the lowest correlations. In the 10 percent of the two-year periods with the highest correlations, the range was 0.56 to 0.78.

These figures suggest that a model with a known correlation of 30 percent is going to look like a model with no information in perhaps one out of six two-year periods (the measured correlation would be less than 0.12). Over a market cycle, however, such a model would probably add value: in 70 percent of the two-year periods the correlations ranged from 0.21 to 0.78.

HOW DATA CAN OVERSTATE POTENTIAL GAINS

Until now the discussion has focused on models with known correlations. In real life, when using model forecasts to make investment decisions, the true forecast correlation is not known. Rather, only an estimate is available. The estimate, moreover, might be overstated by the nature of the data used to create the predictor variables.

Suppose, for example, that on the last day of the month an analyst is trying to create a stock market forecast based on the model described in Chapter 4. The analyst needs to know the level of free reserves for the month. The problem is that the Federal Reserve reports free reserves on a specific day of the week, which may not fall on the last business day of the month. As a result, only an estimate of the level of free reserves is available at month's end. A few days into the next month the Federal Reserve will report the level of free reserves for the previous month. When this occurs the forecast can be updated.

Contrast this operating procedure with the regression model presented in Chapter 4. The predictor variable "free reserves" was downloaded from a database. The regression process knew with perfect hindsight exactly what the level of free reserves was on the last day of each month. This advantage may have lifted the model's reported explanatory power.

Another problem exists because economic data is revised subsequent to its initial release. The Consumer Price Index for the month of January is reported in February. The January figure may or may not be revised in subsequent months. Thus, when

T A B L E   9–3

The Problem of Lost Precision*

	Dec. 1993	Dec. 1992	Dec. 1964	Dec. 1963
CPI in database	145.8	142.0	31.2	30.8
Highest possible figure	145.84	142.04	31.24	30.84
Lowest possible figure	145.75	141.95	31.15	30.75
Actual % change		2.68%		1.30%
Highest possible % change		2.74		1.59
Lowest possible % change		2.61		1.01
Potential error		0.06		0.29

*When the Consumer Price Index is downloaded from a data source, the more current figures typically have four digits but figures for earlier years have only three. As a result, calculations of percent changes are potentially five times less precise for earlier years than they are for later years.

Source: U.S. Department of Labor.

an analyst downloads the CPI for a model, a variable constructed from the CPI could be very different from the same variable created month by month in real time.

Another problem with economic data has to do with rounding. In December 1993 the CPI was 145.8 versus 142.0 in December 1992, according to a database source. In December 1964, meanwhile, the CPI was 31.2 versus 30.8 in December 1963. Notice that the figures for the 1990s have four digits whereas the figures for the 1960s have only three. The year-over-year percent change in the CPI, as a result, is calculated more precisely for the 1990s than it is for the 1960s.

When the CPI was actually released in the 1960s, the figure had four significant digits. The series is periodically rebased to 100, however, leaving figures before the year of adjustment less than 100 and with only three significant digits. Thus, information has been lost about inflation in the earlier years that could mislead the regression process. The potential for lost precision is shown in Table 9–3.[17]

There are ways to approach these data problems. In the case of free reserves, the estimation problem could be solved by using data that is one month older. This would offer a better measure of free reserves, but the data would be stale. So there is a trade-off to consider and a judgment to make: Is fresher data, a bit imperfect, better than more precisely measured data that is a month old?

Another solution is to go through 40 years of biweekly free reserves releases in the business press. Then the series can be created just as it would have been seen month by month over the past 40 years. This approach might also be used in response to the "revision" and "precision" problems with economic data like the Consumer Price Index.

The solution embraced in the models proposed in Section 2 is to try to use prices set in markets, whenever possible. For example, the credit spread variable used in the models, since it is based on month-end yields, is not revised. About one-half of the predictor variables presented in this book are not revised because they are based on market prices. Second, when economic data is used, predictor variables are constructed so that they are not subject to big changes as a result of subsequent revisions. For example, the 12-month change in the CPI is less susceptible to revisions (as a percentage of the value of the variable) than the one- or three-month change in the CPI.

IS SOMETHING DIFFERENT THIS TIME?

There is a third potentially major problem that can reduce the value of model forecasts. Called a *regime shift* by economists, it is essentially a sea change in the patterns that determine asset prices. In the early post–World War II years, for example, stocks yielded as much as 7 percent. A lofty level of income on equities was thought to be necessary compensation for taking on the risk of owning common stocks. In 1950, after all, investors had memories of two world wars and a depression.

But something was different this time. Untold prosperity in the United States and a newfound stability in the world contributed to a repricing of common stocks. By 1960 dividend yields were fluctuating between 3 percent and 4 percent. Stubborn investors waiting for higher payouts missed out on the stock market's 20 percent compound annual return in the 1950s.

The good news with respect to shifts in market pricing regimes is that they occur only rarely. The bad news is that they are difficult to detect until they are well under way, making them an occupational hazard for market timing model makers.

SIMULATING POTENTIAL GAINS FROM MODELS

After considering potential caveats due to chance, data, and shifts in regime, finally we'll try to estimate the potential gains from using the models introduced in Section 2. Recall that the four models presented were estimated through 1993. In order to simulate their potential effectiveness, we now will estimate each model through 1983. Then we will use the model coefficients and data "known" at the close of December 1983 to create a forecast for the market for January 1984. Next, the process will be rolled forward one month, reestimating the model and using data "known" as of January 1984 to make a forecast for February 1984. The word *known* is in quotes above to remind us that some predictor variables being used are subject to the estimation, revision, and precision problems discussed above. Thus we suspect that whatever the estimate of value added is, it may be overstated.[18]

The zero-correlation portfolio for January 1984 was determined by running a parallel regression from 1964 through 1983 without any explanatory variables. This zero-information regression will create a probability forecast for January 1984 that equals the mean historical probability that stocks outperformed Treasury bills over the estimation period. The zero-information regression is then rolled out to January 1984 to determine the zero-correlation portfolio for February 1984.

The simulation process described above makes an attempt at creating forecasts just the way an analyst would have made them in real time going forward. But there is another potential problem that could inflate the estimate of value added over the simulation period.

Suppose a model created in 1993 includes an explanatory variable that an analyst may not have considered had the model been created in 1983. For example, in the early 1980s U.S. financial markets began to pay particular attention to monetary data. For a short time, at the end of each week, market participants eagerly awaited the release of monetary aggregates like M1 and M2. Suppose that the market continued to respond to the monetary data throughout the 1980s. Then an analyst in 1990 might logically have put some measure of monetary aggregates in a model. A simulation over the years from 1980 through 1989 might show that the model worked. But it's probable that, had the analyst created the model in December 1979, the monetary variable would not have been included, because in December 1979 the analyst would not have had 10 years of data showing the relationship between monetary data and the forecast variable. The relationship may hold after 1989, but its fair to say that the results of the simulation over the period from 1980 through 1989 may have been lifted by hindsight bias.

The hindsight bias problem is difficult to remove. When an analyst creates a model, he or she tends to use variables that seem to make sense based on past experience. If the model is developed and estimated over a 30-year period and then simulated over the last 10 years of the 30-year sample, then hindsight bias can creep into the simulation results despite the fact that each simulated forecast was based on information "known at the time." Arguably, such hindsight bias could lift the simulation results that follow.[19]

T A B L E   9–4

Stock Market Model Simulation*

	S&P 500	Zero Correlation Portfolio	Model Portfolio	Model Portfolio Turnover
1984	6.3%	8.0%	13.7%	195%
1985	32.2	20.7	28.5	86
1986	18.5	13.2	15.0	78
1987	5.2	6.2	17.4	87
1988	16.8	12.3	10.6	107
1989	31.5	21.3	23.5	77
1990	−3.2	1.7	2.3	67
1991	30.4	19.6	21.3	82
1992	7.7	6.0	6.0	71
1993	10.0	7.1	6.8	56
Compound annual return	14.9%	11.4%	14.2%	
Standard deviation	15.5%	8.9%	8.7%	
Average annual turnover				90%

*The model portfolio stock exposure equaled the forecast probability that stocks would outperform Treasury bills. The remainder of the model portfolio was allocated to Treasury bills. The zero-correlation portfolio's average allocation was 57 percent stocks/43 percent Treasury bills. The model forecasts had a 0.21 correlation with actual month-ahead excess stock returns.

Source: © *Stock, Bonds, Bills, and Inflation 1996 Yearbook™*, Ibbotson Associates, Chicago (annually updates work by Roger G. Ibbotson and Rex A. Sinquefield). Used with permission. All rights reserved.

SIMULATION RESULTS

That said, we'll get on (finally) with our estimates of potential value added from the models presented in Section 2. The results of the stock market timing model simulation are shown in Table 9–4. For simplicity we used the strategy in which the stock allocation was set equal to the forecast probability P; the percentage invested in Treasury bills equaled 1–P.[20] The model portfolio outperformed the zero-correlation portfolio by 2.8 percentage points a year. The zero-correlation portfolio's average exposure to stocks was 57 percent, reflecting the fact that stocks, on average, outperformed Treasury bills from 1964 through 1993.

Perhaps most noteworthy, the model's excess return potential diminished in the second half of the simulation, probably reflecting a combination of three factors. First, there may have been some erosion in the explanatory power of the model. Second, stock market volatility did decline in the last five years of the simulation to an annualized standard deviation of 12.8 percent versus 17.8 percent in the first five years. The third factor, as discussed earlier in this chapter, is chance. That is, the model's estimated correlation in the first five years may have been slightly higher than the model's true correlation; in the second five years, slightly lower. Unfortunately, the true correlation of a model is never known. The simulation results were roughly in line with expectations, however, so it may well be that the decline in potential value added in the second half of the simulation was due to chance and the drop in stock market volatility, rather than to a permanent erosion in the model's explanatory power.

Now let's consider the bond market model simulation results shown in Table 9–5. The allocation strategy was the same as the one used in the stock market model simulation: The percentage of the portfolio invested in the long-term bonds equaled the probability P that long-term bonds were likely to outperform Treasury bills. The percentage in Treasury bills equaled 1–P.

The model portfolio outperformed the zero-correlation portfolio by 2.6 percentage points a year. The model forecasts, however, had a 0.07 correlation with the next month's excess long bond returns, a relatively low figure. The forecasts, however, had a 0.42 correlation with excess long bond returns over the next six months. The forecasts were only modestly in line with the month-to-month swings in the excess bond returns, but strikingly better predictors over the six-month horizon.

TABLE 9–5

Bond Market Model Simulation*

	Ibbotson Long-Term Government Bond	Zero Correlation Portfolio	Model Portfolio	Model Portfolio Turnover
1984	15.5%	12.3%	14.1%	150%
1985	31.0	18.0	29.7	22
1986	24.5	14.9	23.2	73
1987	−2.7	1.4	−1.3	123
1988	9.7	8.1	6.6	97
1989	18.1	13.2	16.9	45
1990	6.2	7.1	5.3	115
1991	19.4	12.4	16.2	85
1992	7.9	5.9	6.8	55
1993	17.3	10.3	14.6	59
Compound annual return	14.3%	10.3%	12.9%	
Standard deviation	10.3%	5.0%	8.4%	
Average annual turnover				82%

*The model portfolio bond exposure equaled the forecast probability that bonds would outperform Treasury bills. The remainder of the model portfolio was allocated to Treasury bills. The zero-correlation portfolio's average allocation was 49 percent bonds/51 percent Treasury bills. The model forecasts had 0.07 and 0.42 correlations with month-ahead and six-month-ahead excess bond returns, respectively.

Source: © Stock, Bonds, Bills, and Inflation 1996 Yearbook™, Ibbotson Associates, Chicago (annually updates work by Roger G. Ibbotson and Rex A. Sinquefield). Used with permission. All rights reserved.

The model portfolio, on average, was 77 percent invested in long bonds versus 49 percent for the zero-correlation portfolio. The 49 percent figure reflects the fact that there was little to gain from owning long-term bonds relative to Treasury bills throughout a large portion of the period from 1964 through 1993. Broadly speaking, however, the model was right in its assessment that "bonds were undervalued" during most of the simulation period.

TABLE 9-6

Small-Capitalization/Large-Capitalization Relative Performance Simulation*

	Ibbotson Small-Cap	Ibbotson Large-Cap	Zero Correlation Portfolio	Model Portfolio	Model Portfolio Turnover
1984	−6.7%	6.3%	−2.6%	−1.7%	82%
1985	24.7	32.2	27.3	27.5	80
1986	6.9	18.5	11.0	12.6	70
1987	−9.3	5.2	-3.8	3.0	48
1988	22.9	16.8	20.6	14.2	69
1989	10.2	31.5	18.5	23.3	53
1990	−21.6	−3.2	−14.1	−7.9	30
1991	44.6	30.5	38.4	34.8	76
1992	23.3	7.7	16.6	18.3	49
1993	21.0	10.0	16.2	18.2	36
Compound annual return	10.0%	14.9%	11.8%	13.5%	
Standard deviation	17.8%	15.5%	16.2%	15.6%	
Average annual turnover					59%

*The model portfolio small-cap stock exposure equaled the forecast probability that small-cap stocks would outperform large-cap stocks. The remainder of the portfolio was invested in large-cap stocks. The zero-correlation portfolio's average allocation was 60 percent small cap/40 percent large cap. The model forecasts had a 0.10 correlation with the actual month-ahead relative performance between small- and large-cap stocks.

Source: © *Stock, Bonds, Bills, and Inflation 1996 Yearbook™*, Ibbotson Associates, Chicago (annually updates work by Roger G. Ibbotson and Rex A. Sinquefield). Used with permission. All rights reserved.

The small capitalization/large capitalization relative performance model simulation results appear in Table 9–6. The percentage of the portfolio invested in small-cap stocks equaled the forecast probability P that small-cap stocks would outperform large-cap stocks. The remaining percentage of the portfolio, 1–P, was invested in large-cap stocks.

The model portfolio outperformed the zero-correlation port-folio by 1.7 percentage points a year. The model forecasts were 0.10 correlated with the actual month-ahead relative performance between small- and large-cap stocks.

The model was generally underinvested in small-cap stocks during the first seven years of the simulation (average small-cap exposure: 44 percent). In the last three years, however, when small-cap stocks came back into grace, their average expo-sure in the model portfolio rose to 60 percent. The zero-correla-tion portfolio's average allocation was 60 percent small-cap/40 percent large-cap, reflecting the overall good relative perfor-mance of small capitalization stocks from 1970 through 1983.

The Canadian dollar simulation results appear in Table 9–7. Note that the length of the simulation was reduced to 8 years versus 10 for the other three simulations to compensate for a lack of data on the Canadian dollar. The percentage of the model portfolio invested in the Canadian dollar equaled the forecast probability P that the Canadian dollar would rise against the U.S. dollar. The rest of the portfolio was invested in Treasury bills.

It is important to note that, while the regression estimates were based on monthly averages of daily Canadian dollar exchange rates, the simulation used actual month-end-to-month-end returns on the Canadian dollar. A return series was constructed with prices of futures contracts that trade on the Chicago Mercantile Exchange. Each month's Canadian dollar return was based on the percent change of the nearest-to-expi-ration contract on the Canadian dollar. Since an investor who "buys" the Canadian dollar by way of the futures market is allowed to post U.S. Treasury bills to meet margin requirements, the Ibbotson one-month Treasury bill return was added to the return on the futures contract to create an unleveraged total return on the Canadian dollar. Futures prices for the Canadian dollar go back to early 1977.

T A B L E   9–7

Canadian Dollar Model Simulation*

	Canadian Dollar	Zero Correlation Portfolio	Model Portfolio	Model Portfolio Turnover
1986	10.4%	7.0%	6.7%	57%
1987	13.7	7.3	9.8	130
1988	17.6	9.7	17.3	10
1989	14.1	10.6	14.0	30
1990	12.6	9.8	11.6	72
1991	9.0	7.0	7.2	94
1992	−3.4	0.6	2.6	52
1993	1.3	2.4	3.0	43
Compound annual return	9.2%	6.8%	8.9%	
Standard Deviation	4.7%	1.8%	2.9%	
Average annual turnover				61%

*The model portfolio Canadian dollar exposure equaled the forecast probability that the Canadian dollar would out-perform Treasury bills. The remainder of the model portfolio was allocated to Treasury bills. The zero-correlation portfolio's average allocation was 35 percent Canadian Dollar/65 percent Treasury bills. The model forecasts had a 0.21 correlation with actual month-ahead Canadian dollar excess returns. The simulation was limited to eight years because of the lack of historical data.

Sources: © *Stock, Bonds, Bills, and Inflation 1996 Yearbook™*, Ibbotson Associates, Chicago (annually updates work by Roger G. Ibbotson and Rex A. Sinquefield). Used with permission. All rights reserved.
Chicago Mercantile Exchange. Used with permission.

The model portfolio outperformed the zero-correlation portfolio by 2.1 percentage points a year. The model forecasts had a 0.21 correlation with the next month's excess return on the Canadian dollar. The zero-correlation portfolio's average exposure to the Canadian dollar was 35 percent versus 53 percent for the actively managed model portfolio.

10

TURNING MARKET FORECASTS INTO INVESTMENT STRATEGY

EXPLORING SOME APPROACHES TO ASSET ALLOCATION

An investor who has established a long-term or "strategic" asset allocation and has no asset return forecasts has a relatively simple life. The investment portfolio should be continually invested according to the strategic asset allocation schedule. Once an investor has a forecast, however, life becomes more complicated. That's because there are an infinite number of ways to use the information in the forecasts.

Recall that in Chapter 8 the first allocation strategy simulated was one in which the investor was fully invested when the probability that stocks outperform Treasury bills exceeded 50 percent; otherwise, the investor was fully invested in Treasury bills. If we assume that the forecasts have information, the investor's horizon is sufficiently long and transaction costs are sufficiently low, then the active portfolio is going to beat the buy-and-hold alternative.

Many investors, however, might be reluctant to follow such a strategy. The strategy would be fully invested in Treasury bills given a forecast probability of 49 percent and fully invested in stocks if the probability were to rise to 51 percent. The market could rise sharply when the portfolio had no stocks or fall sharply when the portfolio was fully invested. This investor, though seemingly rational, in some respects is willing to take on a lot of risk.

A second investor might want stock exposure to be more closely aligned with forecasts. The portfolio could be fully invested in Treasury bills when forecast probabilities were 50 percent or less. Then, as forecast probabilities rose from 50 percent towards 100 percent, stock exposure could likewise increase gradually from 50 percent to a limit of 100 percent. Still a third investor might choose to maintain a portfolio such that the probability of a loss in any month is kept acceptably low.

Each of the three investment allocation strategies discussed above represents a unique point of view about risk tolerance, that is, the willingness to take on risk in order to achieve return. One way to quantify risk tolerance is to consider what an investor's portfolio would look like in the absence of a short-term forecast. Consider the case of the third investor discussed above, who wanted to maintain a portfolio with a low probability of a loss in any month. Lacking a short-term forecast (which is the same as having a zero-information forecast), this investor probably would maintain a modest investment exposure, since stocks can fall sharply at any time.

Once the investor starts using forecasts, however, investment exposure can deviate from the zero-information, or benchmark portfolio. The magnitude of possible deviations from the benchmark portfolio represents a second element in the description of the investor's risk tolerance. Consider the investor who was 0 percent invested in stocks given a forecast probability less than 50 percent, and who increased exposure to stocks as the probability rose from 50 percent towards 100 percent. The benchmark portfolio might be about 50 percent invested in stocks. The range of exposure to stocks is bounded by 0 percent, when there is a very low forecast, and nearly 100 percent, when the outlook for stocks is exceedingly positive. The investor, however, could have chosen to establish a range from 50 percent short to 150 percent long, or any number of ranges. So there are two parameters to describe an active investor's risk tolerance. First is the benchmark or long-term asset allocation for the portfolio. The second parameter indicates how far the investor is willing to deviate from the benchmark portfolio. An investor who deviates only slightly from the benchmark will earn a return close to the benchmark portfolio performance. An investor who is willing to move far away from the benchmark allocation will outperform the benchmark by a wide margin, assuming the investor is using forecasts with consistently good information.

Table 10–1 shows how the benchmark portfolio can be considered to be a "riskless" portfolio. According to the table, if the benchmark portfolio is 100 percent stocks, then the zero standard deviation or "riskless" portfolio is 100 percent invested in stocks. How can a fully invested portfolio, one that can drop sharply in value at any time, be riskless? It is riskless in the sense that if the investor is 100 percent invested in stocks, performance will not deviate from the 100 percent invested benchmark. True, the portfolio could lose money, but it won't lose money relative to the benchmark.

A riskless portfolio other than Treasury bills is not far-fetched. For example, an investment manager might be paid a performance fee to outperform a stock index. To the extent that the portfolio is underinvested, there is a real risk that the manager will not earn a fee if the market rises sharply.

A bond portfolio also can be a riskless portfolio. Suppose a pension fund has to make fixed annual payments to beneficiaries over the next 10 years. That liability could be perfectly matched by holding 10 zero-coupon bonds, one that matures in

TABLE 10-1

The Benchmark Portfolio as a "Riskless" Portfolio*

Actual Portfolio Stock Exposure	Standard Deviation versus 0% Stock Benchmark	Standard Deviation versus 50% Stock Benchmark	Standard Deviation versus 100% Stock Benchmark
−50%	8.0%	16.0%	24.0%
−40	6.4	14.4	22.4
−30	4.8	12.8	20.8
−20	3.2	11.2	19.2
−10	1.6	9.6	17.6
0 ⟶	0.0	8.0	16.0
10	1.6	6.4	14.4
20	3.2	4.8	12.8
30	4.8	3.2	11.2
40	6.4	1.6	9.6
50	8.0 ⟶	0.0	8.0
60	9.6	1.6	6.4
70	11.2	3.2	4.8
80	12.8	4.8	3.2
90	14.4	6.4	1.6
100	16.0	8.0 ⟶	0.0
110	17.6	9.6	1.6
120	19.2	11.2	3.2
130	20.8	12.8	4.8
140	22.4	14.4	6.4
150	24.0	16.0	8.0

*It is riskless in the sense that if the investor does not deviate from the benchmark portfolio, the portfolio will earn exactly the benchmark return. These figures show the standard deviation of the difference between the actual and benchmark portfolio returns, assuming the standard deviation of stock returns is 16 percent annually.

each of the next 10 years. If interest rates rise, the value of the bond portfolio would fall, but it would be offset exactly by a decline in the present value of the annual benefit payments. From the point of view of the pension fund, that series of zero-coupon bonds is a "risk-free" portfolio. If the pension fund hired a bond manager, then the objective would be to add value relative to the portfolio of 10 zero-coupon bonds, the bench-mark or "risk-free" portfolio.

Once an investor has established a benchmark portfolio, he or she might find it difficult to use forecast probabilities to set investment exposures. Suppose the benchmark is 70 percent stocks/30 percent Treasury bills, and there is a 70 percent probability that stocks will outperform Treasury bills. What should the actively managed portfolio look like?

One way to answer the question is to use the excess return forecast rather than the forecast probability to set investment exposure. The procedure works as follows. First, assume that stocks are going to outperform Treasury bills as they have in the past by seven percentage points a year on average. When the excess return forecast is zero or less, then the portfolio is 100 percent invested in Treasury bills. As the excess return forecast rises from 0 percent to 7 percent, the exposure to stocks is increased in a straight-line fashion. For example, when the excess return is 1 percent, the stock allocation is one-seventh of the fully invested stance; a 2 percent forecast means the portfolio is two-sevenths invested and so on until the portfolio is fully invested. When the forecast exceeds the historical return on stocks, leverage might be allowed up to a 150 percent long position. This allocation schedule is shown in Table 10–2.

This approach is in some ways easier to use than an allocation derived from a forecast probability. To add the most value to an active portfolio, the portfolio should be in Treasury bills or short stocks when the excess return forecast is zero or less. When the forecast lies between zero and the long-term return on stocks, the portfolio's stock exposure should fall between zero and the benchmark allocation. When the forecast exceeds the long-term return on stocks, the portfolio's stock exposure can equal or rise above the benchmark stock allocation.

This method easily accommodates different strategic allocations. Let's go back to the investor whose benchmark was 70 percent stocks/30 percent Treasury bills. If the excess return

T A B L E   10–2

Using the Excess Return Forecast to Set Stock Market Exposure*

Excess Return Forecast	Active Stock Exposure
Less than 0%	0
0	0
1	14%
2	29
3	43
4	57
5	71
6	86
7	100
8	114
9	129
10	143
11	150
More than 11	150

	Active Portfolio	Zero-Correlation Portfolio
Compound annual return	20.8%	12.7%
Annualized standard deviation	16.4%	17.8%
Efficiency ratio (excess return/standard deviation)	0.96	0.43

*The portfolio becomes fully invested as the excess return forecast approaches 7 percent, the long-term excess return on stocks. In this case the investor chose the option of leveraging the portfolio up to 150 percent. The summary returns assume that the stock market returns are normally distributed and have an excess return of 7 percent annually. The risk-free rate is 5 percent and the standard deviation of the stock returns is 16 percent. The forecasts were assumed to have a 30 percent correlation with the next month's stock return. The zero-portfolio average exposure was 106 percent.

forecast is 0 percent or less, the portfolio is fully invested in Treasury bills. As the excess return forecast rises from 0 percent to 7 percent, the portfolio is 10 percent invested for each percentage point increase in the forecast. If the excess return forecast exceeds 10 percent, the investor could use leverage. Likewise, if

TABLE 10–3

The Safety First Criterion*

Excess Return Forecast	First Allocation	Second Allocation
–4%	5%	0
–3	6	0
–2	7	0
–1	9	0
0	11	0
1	15	15%
2	24	24
3	59	59
4	100	100
5	100	100

	First Allocation	Second Allocation	Zero-Correlation Portfolio
Compound annual return	9.0%	9.3%	6.0%
Annualized standard deviation	4.8%	4.7%	2.0%
Efficiency ratio (excess return/standard deviation)	0.82	0.90	0.50

*The first asset allocation schedule is set such that the probability of a loss never exceeds 20%. The rate of investment is gradual and then accelerates as the excess return forecast rises from 0% to 4%. Notice the modest exposure to stocks even when the excess return forecast is less than zero. In the second allocation schedule there is no allocation to stocks when excess return forecast is zero or less, which lifts the resultant efficiency ratio. The average stock exposure for the zero-correlation portfolio was 13%.

the excess return forecast falls below 0 percent, the investor could choose to establish a short position.

A second allocation approach is shown in Table 10–3 in which a criterion called "safety first" is used. In this case the investor wants to maintain as high an exposure to stocks as possible (up to 100 percent) subject to the condition that the probability of a loss in any month never exceeds 20 percent. As the excess return forecasts rise above 0 percent, the probability of a loss quickly diminishes. As a result, investment exposure rises faster than the excess return forecasts. Since portfolio exposure does not rise in a straight line relative to the excess return forecast, there is some loss of efficiency relative to the allocation strategy shown in Table 10–2.[21]

The approach for managing a stocks versus cash portfolio also can be used to manage a bonds versus cash portfolio. In order to execute this strategy for long-term bonds, however, an appropriate risk premium has to be established. According to the Ibbotson figures, long-term government bonds have outperformed Treasury bills by 1.5 percentage points annually from 1926 through 1995. Investors who believe that a 1.5 percent risk premium for bonds is a little low might consider the following approach. Over the same 1926–95 period, the risk premium for stocks was 6.8 percentage points with a standard deviation of 20.4 percent. Meanwhile, the standard deviation of long-term government bonds was 9.2 percent, according to Ibbotson Associates. If we demand from bonds the same efficiency ratio that stocks have offered historically, then we can arrive at a risk premium for long-term government bonds by solving the following equation:

	Stocks		Bonds
$\dfrac{\text{Excess Return}}{\text{Standard Deviation}}$	$\dfrac{6.8\%}{20.4\%}$	$=$	$\dfrac{?}{9.2\%}$

By cross-multiplying and dividing, we find that the appropriate risk premium for long-term government bonds is 3.1 percent. Since we rounded the risk premium for stocks to 7 percent, we will consider 3 percent to be a good number for bonds.

Given agreement on the bond risk premium, the approach to managing a bonds-cash portfolio is the same as managing a stocks-cash portfolio. When the excess return forecast is less than 0 percent, the bonds-cash portfolio is fully invested in Treasury bills and may have a short position in bonds. As the forecast rises from 0 percent to 3 percent, the bond allocation rises from 0 percent to the fully invested stance. When the excess return forecast rises above 3 percent, the portfolio can remain fully invested in bonds or use leverage to buy more bonds.

Until now, we have considered how to manage stocks-cash and bonds-cash portfolios separately. What about using stock and bond market forecasts to manage a single stocks-bonds-cash portfolio? The problem is a bit more complex. That's because with three assets involved the arithmetic gets a little trickier, in part because stock returns are correlated with bond returns.

First, we will consider a naive approach to the three-asset problem that will tend to add value over time. Suppose an investor has established a benchmark portfolio of 60 percent stocks and 40 percent bonds, a typical balanced portfolio. The investor decides that stock exposures can range from 0 percent to 80 percent and bond exposures can range from 0 percent to 60 percent. Funds not invested in stocks or bonds are invested in Treasury bills.

The first step is to set the stock market exposure. If the excess return forecast is zero or less, then the allocation to stocks is zero. For forecasts between 0 percent and the long-term excess return on stocks (we'll continue to use 7 percent), the corresponding stock market exposure would range linearly between 0 percent and 60 percent. If the stock forecast exceeds the long-term excess return on stocks, then the stock allocation can continue to rise with the forecast up to the 80 percent limit. After the stock allocation is made, what is left uninvested is available for investment in bonds. If the excess return forecast on bonds is zero or less, then all of the residual is invested in Treasury bills. For forecasts between zero and the long-term excess return on bonds (recommendation: 3 percent for long-term governments), the bond allocation is set linearly between 0 and 40 percent or the amount of the residual, whichever is less. If the bond forecast exceeds the long-term excess return on bonds, then the bond allocation could range up to the 60 percent maximum, if the funds are available.

While this approach to actively managing a balanced portfolio will tend to add value (assuming the stock and bond forecasts have information), it may not make the most efficient use of the information in the forecasts. For example, if the excess return forecast on stocks was 10 percent and the excess return forecast on bonds was 20 percent, then only 20 percent of the portfolio would be available to take advantage of the screamingly bullish forecast on bonds. One way to solve for that contingency is to set the exposure of bonds first if the excess return forecast on bonds is higher than the excess return forecast on stocks. After the bond exposure is set, what's left is available for stocks.

A SOLUTION TO THE THREE-ASSET ALLOCATION PROBLEM

With the help of a spreadsheet, an investor can solve the three-asset problem precisely. Portfolio theory says that investors associate a measure called *utility*, a sort of mental trade-off between risk and return, with each investment choice. Typically, utility is calculated as the return on an investment less some penalty for the risk associated with the investment. In symbols, we can write

$$U = R - P$$

where

U = Expected utility of the investment.

R = Expected return on the investment.

P = Penalty for the investment's expected risk.

The idea is to calculate the expected utility for all possible investment choices and then choose the investment choice with the highest utility. Note that the utility of the benchmark portfolio is calculated along with all active portfolio utilities. In some cases, the benchmark portfolio will turn out to be the highest utility portfolio.

The expected return on an investment is easy to calculate. In the three-asset case, it is the weighted average of the expected returns on stocks, bonds, and cash:

$$R = W_S R_S + W_B R_B + W_C R_C$$

where

W_S = Percent stocks in the portfolio.
R_S = Expected return on stocks.
W_B = Percent bonds in the portfolio.
R_B = Expected return on bonds.
W_C = Percent cash in the portfolio.
R_C = Expected return on cash.

Each asset weight is multiplied by the asset's expected return. The three products are added together to arrive at the expected return for the portfolio. Note that the three weights must add up to 1 and they are not allowed to take on negative values. This means we are not considering the possibility of selling short or using leverage, although we could if we wanted. In symbols,

$$W_S + W_B + W_C = 1$$

and

$$W_S, W_B, W_C \geq 0$$

Calculating the penalty of an active investment's expected risk is more complicated. First, we break down the penalty P into two components: V, a numerical measure of the investment's risk, and F, a risk penalty factor chosen by the investor. In symbols,

$$P = VF$$

subject to the condition that

$$F \geq 0$$

That is, the risk penalty is the product of the risk measure of an investment portfolio and the risk penalty factor. The risk penalty factor is non-negative.

The risk measure V is the variance of the active portfolio relative to a chosen benchmark portfolio.[22] For a balanced portfolio objective, the benchmark portfolio might be 60 percent stocks and 40 percent bonds. A conservative investor might choose 100 percent cash as a benchmark portfolio. The rules that apply for choosing a benchmark portfolio are the same as those discussed above for choosing an active portfolio. The investment weights are non-negative and they must add up to one.

In symbols, here is how the variance V is calculated:

$$V = (W_{SA} - W_{SB})^2 s_S^2 + (W_{BA} - W_{BB})^2 s_B^2 + 2(W_{SA} - W_{SB})(W_{BA} - W_{BB}) s_S^2 s_B^2 r_{SB}$$

where

W_{SA} = Percent stocks in the active portfolio.
W_{SB} = Percent stocks in the benchmark portfolio.
s_S = Expected standard deviation of stocks.
W_{BA} = Percent bonds in the active portfolio.
W_{BB} = Percent bonds in the benchmark portfolio.
s_B = Expected standard deviation of bonds.
r_{SB} = Expected correlation between stocks and bonds.

In words, the variance V has three components. The first is the square of the difference between the active and benchmark weights in stocks times the square of the expected standard deviation of stocks. Recall that the standard deviation squared is called the variance. This expression says that as the active stock allocation moves further away from the benchmark allocation, the variance between the active and benchmark portfolios increases. Also, as the standard deviation of stocks increases, the variance between the two portfolios increases, assuming the active and benchmark stock allocations are not equal. (If they were equal, the expression would equal zero.) The second component is the same as the first except that it is calculated for bonds instead of stocks.

The third component is twice the product of the difference between the active and benchmark weight in stocks, the difference between the active and benchmark weight in bonds, the expected standard deviation squared (or variance) of stocks, the expected standard deviation squared of bonds, and the expected correlation between stocks and bonds. This is the "tricky" arithmetic associated with the correlation between stocks and bonds. If the correlation is high, then assuming the active stock and bond allocations do not equal the benchmark allocations, this factor's contribution to the overall variance will be high. If the correlation is low, the factor will have little affect. Meanwhile, if the correlation is actually negative, the variance will decline. The reduction in portfolio volatility associated with low or negative correlations between assets is often referred to as a gain from diversification.

To see how diversification can reduce portfolio volatility, consider this example from Elton and Gruber's *Modern Portfolio Theory and Investment Analysis*. Suppose an investor has a choice between two assets, each with three distinct returns based on three possible market outcomes, "good," "average," and "poor," as follows:

Market Outcome	Asset 1 Return	Asset 2 Return	60% Asset 1 40% Asset 2 Return
Good	16%	1%	10%
Average	10%	10%	10%
Poor	4%	19%	10%
Average	10%	10%	10%

The returns range from 4 percent to 16 percent, depending on the market outcome, for asset 1, and from 1 percent to 19 percent for asset 2. If we assume that each market outcome is equally likely, then the expected return of each asset is 10 percent, the average of three returns. Since the assets respond in opposite ways to different market conditions, however, a 60 percent/40 percent split between the two will generate the same return expectation of 10 percent, but with a significant difference. The combination of assets will guarantee a 10 percent return, regardless of market outcome.[23]

Now that we know how to calculate portfolio return and variance for a stocks-bonds-cash portfolio, the next step is to consider the following 10 inputs chosen by the investor:

Benchmark weight stocks

Benchmark weight bonds

Benchmark weight cash

Expected standard deviation stocks

Expected standard deviation bonds

Expected correlation between stocks and bonds

Expected return stocks

Expected return bonds

Expected return cash

Risk penalty factor

in order to find the active weights

Active weight stocks

Active weight bonds

Active weight cash

that correspond to the maximum utility portfolio.[24]

The risk penalty factor determines how far an investor is willing to deviate from the benchmark portfolio. If a risk penalty factor of zero is chosen, then there is no penalty for risk and the portfolio with the highest expected return has the highest utility no matter what the benchmark portfolio is. As the risk penalty factor becomes increasingly positive, holding all other inputs equal, the maximum utility portfolio converges on the benchmark portfolio.

The expected returns on stocks and bonds are determined based on some forecasting process. The expected return on cash is known with certainty based on the current Treasury bill yield.

The expected standard deviations of stock and bond returns, and the expected correlation between stock and bond returns, typically are chosen based on their long-term historical values. The estimates for all three figures will vary, however, depending on which historical period is chosen to be representative of what will happen in the future. Over the 30 years from 1964 through 1993, for example, the standard deviation of stock returns was about 15 percent; of bond returns, about 10 percent. The correlation between the two sets of returns, meanwhile, was about 0.35. Generally speaking, looking further back for estimates results in a higher standard deviation for stocks, a lower figure for bonds, and a lower correlation between stocks and bonds.

As an aside, we will acknowledge that option prices do offer an estimate of market volatility. In general, when investors expect an increase in volatility, option prices go up because heightened volatility increases the odds that the options will be valuable when they expire. So, based on the market price of an option, the so-called implied volatility can be used as an estimate of future volatility. Indeed, *Barron's* magazine publishes the VIX index of implied stock market volatility each week. It is not clear, however, that option prices offer good long-term estimates of volatility, so the approach recommended here is to use a more or less fixed estimate of volatility based on a reasonably long-term (i.e., more than 20 years) historical value.

Back to the spreadsheet. We now know how to calculate the utility of a given active portfolio, assuming that the 10 inputs have been chosen. All that's left is calculating the utility of all portfolios and then finding the portfolio with the highest utility. This "brute force" method could start with a table like the following:

% Stocks	% Bonds	% Cash	Utility
100	0	0	
80	0	20	
80	20	0	
60	0	40	
60	20	20	
60	40	0	
40	0	60	
40	20	40	
40	40	20	
40	60	0	
20	0	80	
20	20	60	
20	40	40	
20	60	20	
20	80	0	
0	0	100	
0	20	80	
0	40	60	
0	60	40	
0	80	20	
0	100	0	

In this case, based on 20 percent increments, the spreadsheet calculates utilities for 21 potential active portfolios. The next step is to sort the four-column block of figures on the utility column to find the portfolio with the highest utility. To improve the precision of a maximum utility portfolio estimate, the number of calculations rises sharply using this method. With a table based on 1 percent increments, the number of portfolios rises to 5,151; on 0.1 percent increments, to 501,501. A spreadsheet designed to calculate 5,151 portfolio utilities can be created since most spreadsheets have at least 8,000 rows.

Of course, well-known numerical methods that dominate the brute force approach both in terms of computer time spent and elegance. Even without the use of those sophisticated techniques, however, someone who is handy with a spreadsheet could arrive at a first rough estimate of the maximum utility portfolio using wide increments. A second, more precise estimate could then be found by working with finer increments in the neighborhood of the first estimate. Such a routine, depending on how it is designed, would reduce computer crunching time and the size of the spreadsheet by a wide margin.

Now that we can determine optimal asset allocations, let's test the assertion made in the Introduction that inputs of return affect portfolio weights more than the volatility and correlation inputs. Consider the following set of asset allocator inputs and the resultant active asset allocation:

Benchmark weight stocks	60%
Benchmark weight bonds	40%
Benchmark weight cash	0%
Standard deviation stocks	16%
Standard deviation bonds	10%
Correlation stocks/bonds	30%
Expected return stocks	12%
Expected return bonds	7%
Expected return cash	5%
Risk penalty factor	6.50
Active allocation stocks	75%
Active allocation bonds	25%
Active allocation cash	0%

We'll start this investigation by allowing the correlation input to range from .10 to .50, leaving the other inputs unchanged, and we'll observe how much the optimal stock allocation changes. Here are the figures:

Correlation	.10	.20	.30	.40	.50
Stocks	72%	73%	75%	77%	80%

In this case, the maximum deviation from the initial 75 percent stock allocation is five percentage points, when the correlation between stocks and bonds rises to 0.50.

Now consider the same exercise, allowing the standard deviation of stocks to range from 12 percent to 20 percent:

Standard deviation	12%	14%	16%	18%	20%
Stocks	82%	78%	75%	72%	70%

In this case, the maximum deviation from the initial 75 percent stock allocation is seven percentage points, when the standard deviation falls to 12 percent.

Finally, we'll repeat this exercise, allowing the expected return on stocks to vary from 8 percent to 16 percent:

Return	8%	10%	12%	14%	16%
Stocks	63%	69%	75%	81%	87%

In this case the maximum deviation from the initial 75 percent stock allocation was the widest of the three, at 12 percentage points, when the expected return is 8 percent and 16 percent.

Now let's consider how other differences in input assumptions prompt changes in recommended asset allocations by our brute force asset allocator. This will help to give us a feel for how the asset allocation process works.

For our first example, suppose an investor has chosen a balanced portfolio of 60 percent stocks and 40 percent bonds as a benchmark portfolio. Expected returns are thought to be in line with historical norms: for stocks, 12 percent; bonds, 7 percent; and cash, 5 percent. Historical norms also are assumed for volatility: a 16 percent standard deviation for stock market returns and 12 percent for bonds. The correlation between stock and bond returns is set at 0.30. All of the figures are shown in Table 10–4.

As the table shows, the investor will be fully invested in stocks if there is no aversion to risk, that is, if the risk penalty is zero. That's because stocks are expected to be the highest return asset under our assumptions, and given no risk aversion, the asset allocator will recommend the portfolio with the highest

T A B L E   10–4

Exploring Portfolio Optimization: Example 1

Benchmark allocation stocks	60%					
Benchmark allocation bonds	40					
Benchmark allocation cash	0					
Standard deviation stocks	16					
Standard deviation bonds	12					
Correlation stocks/bonds	30					
Expected return stocks	12.0					
Expected return bonds	7.0					
Expected return cash	5.0					
Risk penalty factor	0.0	3.0	7.0	15	100	180
Active allocation stocks	100%	89%	73%	66%	61%	60%
Active allocation bonds	0%	11%	27%	34%	39%	40%
Active allocation cash	0%	0%	0%	0%	0%	0%
Standard deviation versus Benchmark	6.8%	4.9%	2.2%	1.0%	0.2%	0.0%

An investor with a balanced portfolio benchmark (60 percent stocks/40 percent bonds) and historically based expected returns, volatility, and correlation will be fully invested in stocks if there is no risk penalty. As the risk penalty rises, the recommended portfolio converges on the benchmark portfolio.

expected return. Remember that the asset allocator is selecting the portfolio with the highest utility. We defined utility as the expected return on a portfolio less a penalty for risk. When there is no penalty for risk the portfolio with the highest utility is simply the portfolio with the highest return.

One drawback to using the risk penalty factor is that it lacks intuitive appeal. Just what does a risk penalty factor of "3" or "7" mean? One way an investor can avoid defining risk tolerance in terms of the risk penalty factor is to choose a level of volatility that the active portfolio will be allowed to have relative to the benchmark portfolio. Given the risk and return assumptions for stocks, bonds, and cash, the investor is essentially asking, "Show me the portfolio with the highest expected

F I G U R E   10–1

"Brute-Force" Asset Allocator
All Portfolios

The settings correspond to those shown in Table 10–4. The benchmark portfolio
(60 percent stocks/40 percent bonds) touches the verticle 0-standard deviation
line. The portfolios running up and to the right show the effect of gradually
reducing the risk penalty factor. When the risk penalty is 0, all funds go to the
highest return asset, in this case, stocks. The northern border of the points from
the benchmark portfolio to the 100 percent stocks portfolio is the efficient frontier.

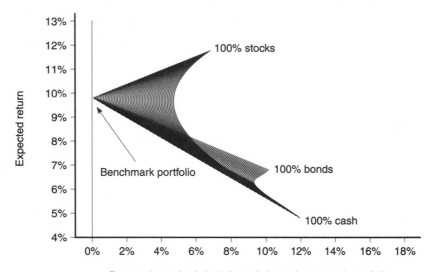

Expected standard deviation relative to benchmark portfolio

return and, say, a 1 percent standard deviation relative to the
benchmark portfolio." Given those specifications, the investor
can try different inputs for the risk penalty factor until the portfolio with a 1 percent standard deviation relative to the benchmark portfolio is found.[25]

Another way to approach selecting the best portfolio is to
plot all possibilities and the so-called efficient frontier. Such a plot
is shown in Figure 10–1 for the asset allocation inputs shown in
Table 10–4. The figure plots active portfolio expected returns

against active portfolio standard deviation. In this case the benchmark portfolio (60 percent stocks/40 percent bonds) touches the vertical 0-standard deviation line. For a sufficiently high risk penalty factor (about 180, according to Table 10–4), the asset allocator will choose the benchmark portfolio. As the risk penalty factor declines, the asset allocator selects portfolios along the efficient frontier, the northernmost line of points in the chart. When the risk penalty factor falls to zero, the asset allocator chooses the highest return portfolio, in this case, 100 percent stocks.

The portfolio furthest down and to the left on the chart is 100 percent cash. While it is clear that cash is the lowest return asset, let's review why it is also the highest risk asset. For purposes of asset allocation, risk is defined relative to the benchmark portfolio. To estimate that risk, we need a column of returns for the benchmark portfolio and a 100 percent cash portfolio. Next, we create a third column by subtracting each portfolio return from the other. The standard deviation of those differences would be 12 percent, according to our assumptions. In words, cash is the highest risk portfolio because it is the most different portfolio, compared to the benchmark 60 percent stocks/40 percent bonds portfolio.

In our second example we will consider an investor whose benchmark portfolio is 100 percent cash. This investor does not want to own bonds; the portfolio will be shifted between stocks and cash as expectations for stock returns change. To exclude bonds from consideration, an expected return of –99.9 percent was input for that asset. As shown in Table 10–5, when the expected return on stocks equals the return on cash, the investor holds no stocks. That's because there is no added compensation relative to holding cash for taking on the risk of owning stocks. As the expected return on stocks rises, however, the allocation to stocks increases in straight-line fashion. This investment strategy is exactly analogous to one discussed earlier in this chapter and shown in Table 10–2.

T A B L E   10-5

Exploring Portfolio Optimization: Example 2

Benchmark allocation stocks	0%							
Benchmark allocation bonds	0							
Benchmark allocation cash	100							
Standard deviation stocks	16							
Standard deviation bonds	12							
Correlation stocks/bonds	30							
Expected return stocks	5%	6%	7%	8%	9%	10%	11%	12%
Expected return bonds	−99.9%							
Expected return cash	5.0%							
Risk penalty factor	5.00							
Active allocation stocks	0%	14%	29%	43%	58%	72%	87%	100%
Active allocation bonds	0%	0%	0%	0%	0%	0%	0%	0%
Active allocation cash	100%	86%	71%	57%	42%	28%	13%	0%
Standard deviation versus Benchmark	0.0%	2.2%	4.6%	6.9%	9.3%	11.5%	13.9%	16.0%

*An investor with a 100 percent cash benchmark will be fully invested in cash if the expected return on stocks is less than or equal to the return on cash. As the expected return on stocks rises, the allocation to stocks increases proportionately. This investor chooses not to invest in bonds at all times. To exclude bonds from consideration, a very low expected return was input for bonds.

The third example we will consider is of an investor with no risk aversion (risk penalty factor = 0) and a 100 percent stocks benchmark. Notice in Table 10–6 that if the expected return on stocks is slightly lower than the return on cash, then the investor is fully invested in cash. If the expected return on stocks rises only slightly above the return on cash, however, the investor becomes fully invested in stocks. This investment approach is exactly the same as the strategy detailed in Table 8–3.

A final example has the following inputs:

Benchmark weight stocks	60%
Benchmark weight bonds	40%
Benchmark weight cash	0%

T A B L E   10–6

Exploring Portfolio Optimization: Example 3

Benchmark allocation stocks	100%	
Benchmark allocation bonds	0	
Benchmark allocation cash	0	
Standard deviation stocks	16	
Standard deviation bonds	12	
Correlation stocks/bonds	30	
Expected return stocks	4.9%	5.1%
Expected return bonds	−99.9%	
Expected return cash	5.0%	
Risk penalty factor	0.00	
Active allocation stocks	0%	100%
Active allocation bonds	0%	0%
Active allocation cash	100%	0%
Standard deviation versus benchmark	16.0%	0.0%

This investor has a 100 percent stocks benchmark and an infinite tolerance for risk (risk penalty factor = 0). When the expected return on stocks is less than the return on cash, then the portfolio is fully invested in cash. If the expected return on stocks rises above the return on cash, then the portfolio is fully invested in stocks. This strategy was discussed in Chapter 8. Simulated returns for the strategy are shown in Table 8–3.

Standard deviation stocks	15%
Standard deviation bonds	10%
Correlation stocks/bonds	30%
Expected return stocks	4.8%
Expected return bonds	1.6%
Expected return cash	5.1%

Given this problem set, the optimal active portfolio with a 2.5 percent standard deviation against the benchmark portfolio has the following weights:

Stocks	64%
Bonds	14%
Cash	22%

As expected, the active allocation to bonds is well below the benchmark allocation, owing to their low expected return. Note, however, that the active stock allocation is slightly above the benchmark allocation despite the fact that the expected return on stocks is less than the return on cash. As already noted, the optimizer doesn't like bonds. But there also is disdain for cash because cash is not included in the benchmark portfolio.

Meanwhile, stocks are expected to do better than bonds and almost as well as cash. Moreover, stocks are assumed to be correlated with bonds. In a sense, then, owning stocks is something like owning bonds. So the optimizer is using a few percentage points of stocks as a partial bond substitute in an attempt to offset the risk taken against the benchmark by sharply cutting back on bonds. If stocks had been assumed to have no correlation with bonds, then the active stock allocation would not have exceeded the benchmark allocation. If a correlation greater than 30 percent had been input, then the optimizer would have put even more stocks in the active portfolio.

Some readers no doubt will want to be able to solve more complicated asset allocation problems. For example, what if a fourth asset, such as European stocks, is added to the mix? What if an investor has constraints such as a minimum required income? Many asset allocation software programs on the market address these additional issues. A few of them are listed in Appendix 3.

OTHER APPROACHES TO MARKET TIMING AND CONCLUDING REMARKS

11

THREE WALL STREET STRATEGIES

In this chapter we will investigate three other approaches to forecasting financial markets and the implementation of investment strategy based on the forecasts. Although each approach could in theory be formulated for any financial market, all three are in fact designed to forecast the stock market.

There are two major criteria for choosing the methodologies. First, all three have been practiced by a prominent Wall Street strategist for nearly two decades. Second, each strategy has a well-defined process for creating forecasts and an established discipline for setting investment strategy based on the forecasts.

Broadly speaking, what separates the three methods of forecasting the stock market is the manner in which the explanatory variables are chosen. The first investment strategy might best be described as a multi-indicator approach. Practiced by Martin Zweig, it is about as close as one can get to a purely empirical method of forecasting the stock market. Edward Kerschner of Paine Webber focuses on investor expectations of corporate dividends, earnings, and earnings growth rates, which makes his approach purely fundamental. Elaine Garzarelli looks at indicators, but she also emphasizes analyzing corporate profits. Thus, her approach combines the empirical and the fundamental.

Does this mean that Martin Zweig doesn't care about earnings growth rates? Or that Edward Kerschner never looks at the level of commercial paper outstanding? Nonsense. Indeed, although each strategist has a well-defined core process for making forecasts, all of them consider other factors from time to time in the ongoing analysis of the stock market.

MARTIN ZWEIG—CHAMPION OF THE INDICATORS

Owing to his frequent appearances on the PBS series *Wall Street Week* and his popular market newsletter *The Zweig Forecast*, Martin Zweig is perhaps the most widely recognized of the three market strategists reviewed in this chapter. Broadly categorized here as an "empiricist," Zweig is willing to consider a wide range of factors that might prove useful in forecasting the stock market. Indeed, he makes use of the time-honored hyperbole when he writes that

> Most people think of me as a technician, but actually, I use anything that works. If they worked, I'd track the planets or sunspots, or even use a Ouija board.

As it turns out, "what works" are factors that can be grouped into three broad categories, the most important being the monetary environment. Indeed, Zweig continues, *"the major direction of the market is dominated by monetary considerations, primarily Federal Reserve policy and the movement of interest rates* (italics his)."[26]

Based on this research outcome, Zweig maintains an index of 22 interest rate and Federal Reserve indicators. Called the Monetary Model, the index can take on values between 0 and 100. Roughly speaking, a reading above 65 has bullish implications for the stock market and readings below 35 are considered bearish. Readings in between are described as moderately bullish (approximately 60–65), somewhat positive or high neutral (55–59), neutral (46–54), somewhat negative or low neutral (41–45), and moderately bearish (35–40).

Zweig does not disclose all of his indicators, and from time to time he adds, deletes, or modifies some. He has cited several monetary indicators over the years, however, including the Prime Rate Indicator, the Fed Indicator, the Installment Debt Indicator, free reserves, government and corporate bond yields, and commercial paper outstanding. Some indicators are calculated in a rather simple manner such as taking the one-year percent change in the one-year Treasury bill yield. Others are calculated based on a more complex set of rules. The rules for constructing the Fed Indicator, for example, involve the timing and direction of changes in reserve requirements and the discount rate. (The discount rate is the interest rate charged on loans from the Federal Reserve to banks. Reserve requirements, also set by the Federal Reserve, affect the ease with which banks can make loans to businesses and individuals.)[27]

Zweig analyzes some indicators by devising buy and sell rules and then considering a hypothetical investor who was 100 percent long stocks when the buy signals were in place and was 100 percent invested in cash equivalents for the duration of the sell signals. Other indicators are tested by creating categories such as bullish, neutral, moderately bearish, and outright bearish. The stock market's return is then calculated for each category over the period of the test. For example, if an indicator was bullish from time to time for a total of 11 years over a 30-year test period, then a hypothetical compound annual return is calculated for the bullish periods as if they were one contiguous 11-year period.

Notice that the categories in the above example were not symmetric: there was a moderately bearish category but none labeled moderately bullish. The lack of symmetry means that the stock market can be tested for its nonlinear response to changes in an indicator. In the extreme, stock market performance could be average over 80 percent of the range of an indicator (when it might be assigned a score of 0) but excellent in the remaining 20 percent of the range (when it might take on a score of 1).

Based on the various tests, Zweig assesses the reliability of each indicator. Roughly speaking, the more reliable an indicator, the more weight it will receive in the construction of a composite index. For example, in an index of two indicators, the stronger indicator might receive a score from 0 to 20; the weaker, a score from 0 to 5. The index, calculated as the sum of the two scores, ranges from 0 to 25. Clearly, the stronger indicator carries more weight than the weaker indicator.

The Monetary Model is complemented by two other broad categories of indicators: momentum and sentiment. Stock market momentum can be likened to inertia, the tendency of a body in motion to stay in motion. Likewise, a rising stock market often continues to rise and buying a market in decline can turn out to be like trying to catch a falling knife. Hence Zweig's famous lines, "the trend is your friend" and "don't fight the tape."

One measure of stock market momentum is based on the number of advancing and declining issues on the New York Stock Exchange (the Advance/Decline Line); a second momentum indicator is the ratio of the number of shares traded of stocks that rise on a given day divided by the number of shares traded of stocks that decline (the Up Volume Indicator). Both of these measures of "tape action" try to gauge the health of the market by asking how individual stocks, from large to small, are doing, as opposed to looking at a narrowly based stock market index such as the Dow Jones Industrial Average or even the Standard & Poor's index of 500 stocks, the **S&P 500.** The Four Percent Model flashes a buy signal when the Value Line Composite Index rises 4 percent or more above a previous weekly market low and remains in a buy mode until the index falls from any subsequent weekly peak 4 percent or more. Two other momentum indicators that Zweig cites from time to time are the number of weekly new highs on the New York Stock Exchange and the number of weekly new lows.

Sentiment indicators measure the degree of optimism or pessimism in the market. Monitoring sentiment is useful, according to Zweig, because extremes in sentiment often signal a change in market direction: extreme optimism often warns of a top; extreme pessimism, a market bottom.

Some of the more important sentiment indicators are the Mutual Funds Cash-to-Assets Ratio (low cash holdings indicating optimism) and whether investment advisors' opinions, in the aggregate, are bullish or bearish. A similarly constructed sentiment indicator tabulates the number of bullish and bearish stock index future traders. Note that Zweig only monitors the above sentiment indicators; they are calculated and distributed by a third party. One sentiment indicator unique to Zweig, the *Barron's* Ads Indicator, compares the number of bullish to bearish advertisements in that financial newspaper, published weekly by Dow Jones & Co. As with virtually all sentiment indicators, a preponderance of bullishness (optimism) often signals trouble ahead, and vice versa.

In sum, Zweig has a Monetary Model, which has roughly a 50 percent weight in determining stock market exposure, momentum indicators (about 20 percent) and sentiment indicators (about 30 percent). Zweig combines 36 momentum and sentiment indicators in all to form the Intermediate Index. Scores for the Monetary Model and the Intermediate Index are published every three weeks and are updated frequently on a telephone hotline service.

As for translating model scores into investment strategy, Zweig's approach is pretty straightforward. When the Monetary Model and the Intermediate Index together are bullish, Zweig is not shy about being fully, or at least nearly fully invested. Likewise, when the indicators are bearish, he will recommend little if any exposure to the stock market, and may even recommend purchasing some put options. Broadly speaking, as the indicators rise from bearish to bullish, recommended stock market exposure rises from virtually zero to a fully invested stance. True to his emphasis on flexibility, Zweig occasionally recommends a stock market exposure that is up to 15 percentage points more or less than his indicators, taken alone, would imply.

From mid-1980 through 1992, *The Zweig Forecast* outperformed nearly all of its competitors, according to the *Hulbert Financial Digest*, a service that rates investment advisory newsletters. Indeed, according to Hulbert, an investor who followed Zweig's recommendations would have outperformed the S&P 500 by about 1.5 percentage points a year in that period from the 1980s to the early 1990s.

Zweig's achievement is all the more impressive when we consider that his average stock market exposure is well below 100 percent. Recall that in order to gauge the effectiveness of an investment strategy, one must first establish a benchmark portfolio that represents an investor's stance, given a neutral forecast. An analysis of *The Zweig Forecast* shows that when the Monetary Model and the Intermediate Index were in neutral territory, the recommended stock market exposure was about 65 percent. Thus, the performance of the newsletter arguably should be compared to a portfolio composed of 65 percent stocks and 35 percent cash. As it turns out, Martin Zweig's advisory service outperformed the more appropriately constructed benchmark portfolio by approximately four percentage points (17.4 percent versus 13.4 percent) from mid-1980 through the close of 1992.[28]

EDWARD KERSCHNER—DEFENDER OF FUNDAMENTALS

Edward Kerschner has published monthly forecasts of the relative attractiveness of stocks, bonds, and cash equivalents in a piece called *Asset Allocation/Equity Selection* for Paine Webber since December 1972. Over that 20-plus-year period an investor who followed the stock market forecasts would have beat the stock market, a balanced portfolio aligned with the forecasts would have outperformed its benchmark, and a flexibly run portfolio would have outperformed the best performing asset (stocks) by more than two percentage points a year while taking on a little more than half the risk associated with equities.

In order to forecast the stock market, Kerschner starts by polling institutional investors about their expectations for the current level of earnings and dividends and earnings growth rates.[29] These figures are *normalized*, that is, adjustments are made to the numbers if they are unusually high or low. For example, at the bottom of a recession, earnings could be at a cyclical low and investors may well expect them to rise sharply as an economic recovery unfolds. In that case, the level might be increased to reflect nonrecessionary earnings power and the growth rate might be reduced to something more sustainable.

We have to consider a little financial theory to see how expectations about earnings, dividends, and growth rates can be translated into forecasts. The first concepts to cover are future value and present value.

Future value is relatively easy to handle. If an investor puts $100 into a bond that pays the original $100 plus a single 10 percent interest payment a year later, the future value of the investment is $110. We could calculate the future value by starting with the $100 and multiplying by 1.10. The "1" in 1.10 represents the fact that the original investment will be returned—the original investment, $100, equals $1 \times \$100$. The ".10" represents the 10 percent interest on the investment.

If the $110 is reinvested at the same rate for a second year, the future value at the close of year two is

$$\$110 \times 1.10 = \$121$$

Now, suppose someone invests $100 for two years at 10 percent a year. Assuming the first interest payment is reinvested at 10 percent, the future value of the investment is

$$\$100 \times 1.10 \times 1.10 =$$
$$\$100 \times (1.10)^2 = \$121$$

By extension, it's easy to see that the multiplier to find the future value for the same investment over three years is $(1.10)^3 = 1.33$. And so on.

To get at present value, all we have to do is think about future value in reverse. If an investor is going to get $110 a year from now and the investor's expected interest rate is 10 percent, then the present value of the money to be received in the future is $100. The calculation is just the opposite of the future value calculation. That is, the present value is

$$\$110/1.10 = \$100$$

Likewise, if the expected interest rate is 10 percent, and the investor will receive $121 two years from now, then the present value is

$$\$121/(1.10 \times 1.10) =$$
$$\$121/(1.10)^2 = \$100$$

Again, by extension, if the expected rate of return is 10 percent, the divisor to find the present value of a cash payment received in three years is $(1.10)^3$. [29]

Now suppose an investor is going to get $20 at the close of year one, $30 at the close of year two and $40 at the close of year three. If the investor's expected rate of return is 10 percent, then the present value of those three cash flows is

$$\frac{\$20}{(1.10)} + \frac{\$30}{(1.10)^2} + \frac{\$40}{(1.10)^3} =$$

$$\$18.18 + \$24.79 + \$30.05 = \$73.02$$

Based on this process, given an expected rate of return, the present value of any series of cash flows can be calculated.

Now, according to financial theory, the price of a stock can be thought of as the present value of its dividends. The dividends are the cash flows and investors, in the aggregate, determine the expected rate of return.

In order to calculate the present value of the dividends, a simplifying assumption is made, namely, that they will grow forever at a constant rate. If that is the case, then the present value of the dividends, that is, the price of the stock, is

$$P = \frac{D}{(1 + r)} + \frac{D(1 + g)}{(1 + r)^2} + \frac{D(1 + g)^2}{(1 + r)^3} + \frac{D(1 + g)^3}{(1 + r)^4} \cdots$$

where

P = The price of the stock.

D = The dividend received at the end of year one.

g = The constant dividend growth rate.

r = The expected rate of return.

It turns out that the right-hand side of the expression is an infinite series that can be simplified so that the equality becomes

$$P = \frac{D}{(r - g)}$$

Recall that, based on his survey, Kerschner determines the normalized dividend (D) and earnings growth rate (g) for the stock market as a whole. If we assume that, on average, companies will pay out a constant percentage of earnings as dividends, then the earnings and dividend growth rates will be equal. We can find the price (P) of the market in the newspaper. That leaves a little algebra to solve for r, the expected rate of return. Indeed, the expected rate of return

$$r = \frac{D}{P} + g$$

Some readers will notice that (D/P) is the dividend yield. So, given the assumptions of the so-called constant growth dividend discount model, the expected rate of return equals the dividend yield (calculated as next year's dividend divided by the current stock market price) plus the constant growth rate.

Happily, finding the expected rate of return for bonds and cash equivalents is a lot less involved than finding the expected rate of return for stocks. For bonds, it is defined as the 10-year constant maturity Treasury yield; for cash equivalents, the yield on newly issued three-month Treasury bills. Both figures are published by the Federal Reserve.

After the expected returns for stocks, bonds, and cash are determined, the next step is to compare the current relationship among the three to the average over the past 20 years. If, for example, the difference between the expected rates of return on stocks and cash is higher than the historical average, then an investor is getting more now to invest in stocks relative to cash. Likewise, the current relationship between stocks and bonds is compared to the historical relationship, and bonds are similarly compared to cash. Based on the difference between the current and the historical, the relative attractiveness of stocks, bonds, and cash is determined.

The final step, based on the relative attractiveness of the three assets, is to create model portfolios. Kerschner publishes suggested equity account weights where stocks can range from 0 percent to 100 percent of the portfolio and up to 25 percent can be invested in cash equivalents. Kerschner also offers a suggested balanced portfolio in which stocks can range from 40 percent to 100 percent, bonds can range from 10 percent to 75 percent, and cash equivalents can range from 0 percent to 25 percent. And he constructs a final "flexible" portfolio such that the allocation to stocks equals the probability that stocks will outperform both bonds and cash. Likewise, the bond allocation equals the probability that bonds will outperform stocks and cash; the cash allocation equals the probability that cash will outperform stocks and bonds.

Kerschner's work is compelling for two reasons. First, as said earlier, an investor who followed his readily documentable forecasts would have generated excellent excess returns from the early 1970s to present. Second, Kerschner's investment process is firmly supported by financial theory. Thus, there is good reason to believe it will continue to add value.

ELAINE GARZARELLI—FUSION FORECASTER

While it is fair to characterize Elaine Garzarelli's approach to forecasting the stock market as a hybrid of the fundamental and technical/indicator approaches, the bulk of her value-added work is in the fundamental realm. Indeed, her roots are in the fundamental rather than the technical.

As a young analyst in the mid-1970s, Garzarelli forged industry earnings models for the now-defunct Becker Securities, Inc. The models integrated industrywide factors with factors that affected the overall economy to arrive at profits for each industry. For example, the model for the steel industry used recent cash flow and capacity utilization for the companies (industry factors) as an input for estimating capital spending. Meanwhile, the unemployment rate and unit labor costs for nonfinancial corporations (economywide factors) were used as inputs to estimate labor costs. Garzarelli continues to use similarly constructed models in her work today.

A second theme of her early work at Becker was investigating how earnings and other fundamental factors could be used to forecast industry and individual stock price performance. The idea was to look at a fundamental factor such as sales for an industry and compare it to sales for the S&P index of 400 industrial companies. The relative concept was executed by dividing industry sales by the sum of sales for the 400 companies that made up the index. If the ratio was increasing, then the industry in question was outperforming the S&P 400; likewise, a decline in the ratio meant that industry sales were lagging the overall market. Correlations were calculated between relative price performance and each of several fundamental factors.

From those beginnings, Garzarelli moved on to Shearson Lehman Brothers, where her research manifested itself in *Sector Analysis Monthly Monitor*, a publication dedicated to forecasting relative industry price performance and the outlook for the stock market. Recently she left Shearson to set up her own shop, appropriately named Garzarelli Capital.

In order to gauge the outlook for the stock market, Garzarelli monitors 14 stock market indicators, each of which is scored as having a negative, neutral, or positive influence on the stock market. The indicators are divided into four groups: economic cycle, monetary, valuation, and sentiment. Each group contributes approximately 25 points to a composite score that ranges from 0 to 100.

Garzarelli's system records a buy signal when the indicators reach 65 or higher. Once a buy signal is established, it remains in place until the score falls to 20 or below, an event that would trigger a sell recommendation. The indicators would then remain in sell territory until they rise again to 65 or higher.

Garzarelli uses three economic cycle indicators: S&P 500 earnings momentum, economic output momentum, and the coincident to lagging indicators ratio. *Momentum* refers to percent change over a year's time. The S&P 500 earnings are adjusted for nonrecurring events, such as a write-off, that often distort the profit picture. Industrial production (a monthly Federal Reserve measure of the output of the manufacturing and mining sectors and the electric utility industry) is used as a proxy for economic output.

The coincident and lagging indicators are indexes published monthly by the U.S. Department of Commerce along with the index of leading economic indicators. The components of the coincident index, such as industrial production, tend to peak and trough at approximately the same time as overall economic activity peaks and troughs. Likewise, components of the leading index, such as stock prices, tend to peak and trough in advance of peaks and troughs in overall economic activity. Finally, components of the lagging index, such as the average prime rate charged by banks, tend to lag overall economic activity.[30]

It turns out that Garzarelli prefers the ratio of coincident to lagging indicators over the leading indicators for forecasting turning points in economic output. Indeed, Garzarelli has written that the ratio of coincident to lagging indicators is the "best leading indicator of the economy."[31]

Garzarelli analyzes the economic cycle indicators roughly as follows. Shortly before a bottom in S&P earnings momentum, stocks tend to rise; likewise, shortly before a peak in earnings momentum, stock prices often begin to decline. Stock prices similarly rise (fall) before troughs (peaks) in economic output momentum. A peak (trough) in the coincident to lagging indicators ratio has a negative (positive) influence on stock prices.

The monetary group has seven indicators, two of which are major in the sense that they can add significantly to the overall score; the other five together contribute modestly.

The first of the two major indicators is the trend in three-month Treasury bill rates. Rising Treasury bill rates generally have a negative influence on stock prices. Indeed, a rise 20 percent to 25 percent above a cyclical low often results in a 10 percent to 15 percent stock market correction, according to Garzarelli. As might be expected, a decline in short-term rates is bullish for stocks.

The second of the major monetary indicators is the relationship between the three-month Treasury bill rate and the discount rate. When the Treasury bill rate is above the discount rate (again, the rate charged by the Federal Reserve for temporary loans to banks), stocks tend to perform poorly. Likewise, when the Treasury bill rate is below the discount rate, stocks tend to do well.

This indicator may work because Treasury bill rates are set freely by market forces, while the discount rate is set by the Federal Reserve. When the Treasury bill rate is above the discount rate, the Federal Reserve may have to play catch-up by raising the discount rate or by taking some other tightening action, a potential negative for stocks. The process works in reverse when Treasury bill rates are below the discount rate.

The five minor monetary indicators include free reserves, interest rate momentum, the yield curve, money supply momentum, and the so-called liquidity ratio. Positive free reserves, declining interest rate momentum, a positive yield curve, and rising money supply momentum are generally good for stocks and vice versa. The liquidity ratio is calculated by starting with the level of the money supply as measured by M3 and adjusting it for inflation by dividing by the Consumer Price Index. That figure is adjusted one step further by dividing by the level of industrial production. The resultant figure, when it is rising, indicates that the real money supply is growing faster than real economic output, or that liquidity is rising. This tends to be positive for stocks. A fall in the index, meaning that systemwide liquidity is on the decline, tends to be negative for stocks.

The first of two valuation indicators looks at the relationship between cash flow and the average of the three-month and 30-year Treasury issue yields. Cash flow is calculated by adding noncash expenses to reported profits to estimate how much money actually enters or leaves a company's coffers over the course of a reporting period. The so-called cash flow yield is cash flow for the S&P 500 divided by the S&P 500 index itself. When the cash flow yield falls to an unsustainably low level chosen on the basis of historical norms, it generates a sell signal; likewise, when the cash flow yield rises to a certain point, the indicator is in buy territory.

The second valuation indicator uses regression-based forecasts of the price earnings ratio, given the current economic environment. When the P/E ratio forecast is higher than the current P/E, then stocks are likely to rise, and vice versa.

The two sentiment indicators are mutual and switch fund cash levels, and the percentage of bullish advisors (*switch funds* are market timing advisory services that recommend switching back and forth from equity to money market mutual funds). Both sentiment indicators take on the usual significance. Low cash levels mean that managers and advisors are bullish, a poor sign for stocks. Likewise, when the percentage of bullish advisors is unusually high, stocks tend to do poorly.

Although a real time record of Garzarelli's stock market timing methodology is not readily available, she does publish simulated or "backtested" buy and sell signals for the indicators from 1969 to present. Recall that simulations can overstate potential gains from executing a market timing strategy. Interestingly, a simulation of an approach like Garzarelli's has an added layer of uncertainty.

In Chapter 9 we observed that, owing to data revisions, a model often "sees" an information set in a simulation that is slightly different from what would have been seen in real time. Now observe that Garzarelli's methodology requires *forecasts as inputs for making forecasts*. For example, peaks and troughs in earnings and industrial production momentum are forecast for two of the economic cycle indicators. It is possible that a simulation of a methodology like this one will "see" perfect forecasts that in real time could not be perfect.

That said, Garzarelli's stock market indicators nevertheless do bear watching. If we assume an investor was fully invested in equities when buy signals were in place and fully invested in Treasury bills when the indicators were in sell territory, an investor would have outperformed the S&P 500 by about six percentage points annually from 1969 through 1995.

12

CONCLUDING REMARKS

Certainly there are ways to improve upon the market timing process described in this book. Let's consider some potentially useful avenues for further research by reexamining a few of the simplifying assumptions made regarding implementation.

One such assumption was the timing of investment decisions, which were limited to the last day of the month. There are times when the action of predictor variables guarantees a significant change in a forecast well before month's end. When this occurs, a market timer is free to make intramonth portfolio adjustments. Whether to make such an investment decision, moreover, doesn't have to be done on an ad hoc basis. That's because today's econometric software packages can handle daily and weekly data as well as the normal monthly, quarterly, and annual frequencies. Indeed, it is possible to mix the frequency of predictor variables within a single model. For example, interest rates could be recorded daily; initial unemployment claims, weekly; free reserves, biweekly; and industrial production, monthly for a model that produces updated forecasts as often as daily.

Some investors may decide not to venture away from a strategic asset allocation unless a forecast comes along that points to significant mispricing. This approach may be appealing to a large number of equity investors for two reasons. First, stocks have trended upward over time. Second, market cycles typically are composed of a bull phase followed by a shorter bear phase. As a result, some investors are reluctant to try to time shorter term swings in the market. Of course, there is no rule that the stock market has to trend upward and that bull markets are neatly followed by shorter duration bear markets. Indeed, as we enter the 21st century, market watchers looking back may observe that investors of the mid-1990s were lulled into believing that short-lived bear markets and reduced volatility were the rule rather than the exception. Hence, the incremental approach (an approach in which small portfolio adjustments are made in response to ongoing forecasts) may prevail over an approach in which portfolio adjustments are made only occasionally when forecasts are extremely bullish or bearish.

Another approach for improving the models proposed in Section 2 is to combine their forecasts with forecasts from other models. For example, each of Zweig's, Garzarelli's, and Kerschner's principal tools for forecasting go back a minimum of nearly 20 years, a reasonable time frame for testing a composite model. Rather than creating a single "super model," an analyst would probably prefer to maintain the models as separate entities. That's because a market timer may not be able to duplicate the work of several market strategists or find it too expensive to do so. Moreover, even if the work could be duplicated, some analysts might argue that such a super model would be unmanageable because it probably would have dozens of explanatory variables.

Another more technical modification to the models is to investigate potential gains from relaxing the normality assumption. In the case of stocks, one important deviation from normality is the prevalence of extreme movements. It is true that very large percentage changes in stock prices would be possible if they were normally distributed. Such changes occur frequently enough, however, that many researchers have questioned the normality assumption. One obvious drawback to this approach is that the simplicity of the normal distribution is lost. A second drawback is that there is no consensus on the best way to model the nonnormality of stock returns. One final observation regarding this idea: Even assuming that a better estimate of the distribution of stock returns could be found, such an improvement is no substitute for a good forecast.

A final approach offering tremendous potential is to model additional asset classes. In addition to the U.S. fixed income and equity markets, there are international counterparts. Emerging markets might be modeled separately from the markets of the more mature industrialized countries. Clearly, there are opportunities in modeling currencies and commodities. Finally, modeling spreads (like small versus large stocks) might prove to add value. For example, an analyst might fail in modeling the soybean market, but find a meaningful relationship for forecasting changes in the difference between soybean and soybean oil prices. As more forecasts are added, opportunities to take advantage of mispriced assets will become more frequent. Moreover, gains from diversification will be achieved as a market timer's designated set of investable assets grows in number.

Mechanics of a Regression

In this example, X_1, X_2 and X_3 for each year are used to forecast Y in the following year. The regression was estimated from 1977 through 1993. Since each Y was run against the Xs from the previous year, the Xs used to estimate the regression run from 1976 through 1992.

The forecasts equal the constant plus (X_1 times coefficient X_1) plus (X_2 times coefficient X_2) plus (X_3 times coefficient X_3). The 1977 forecast equals $.48 + (.08 \times 1.54) + (.94 \times -3.22) + (.94 \times 3.86) = 1.20$. The forecast for 1994 is an out-of-sample forecast because the relationship from 1977 through 1993 was used to forecast Y for 1994.

The residuals equal the actual value of Y for the year less the forecast for the same year.

Year	Y	X_1	X_2	X_3	In-Sample Forecast	Residual
1976	1.15	0.08	0.94	0.94		
1977	1.54	0.25	0.74	0.79	1.20	0.34
1978	1.64	0.83	0.79	0.84	1.53	0.11
1979	2.40	0.73	0.41	0.51	2.46	−0.06
1980	1.97	0.32	0.89	1.00	2.25	−0.28
1981	1.65	0.16	0.08	0.25	1.97	−0.32
1982	1.32	0.32	0.83	0.87	1.43	−0.11
1983	1.40	0.60	0.54	0.68	1.66	−0.26
1984	2.58	0.48	0.98	1.00	2.29	0.29
1985	1.72	0.05	0.33	0.41	1.92	−0.20
1986	1.21	0.76	0.94	1.09	1.08	0.13
1987	3.26	0.10	0.33	0.36	2.83	0.43
1988	1.09	0.58	0.31	0.40	0.96	0.13
1989	1.83	0.89	0.25	0.36	1.92	−0.09
1990	2.54	0.66	0.10	0.11	2.44	0.10
1991	1.51	0.08	0.64	0.78	1.60	−0.09
1992	1.35	0.29	0.03	0.07	1.55	−0.20
1993	1.25	0.41	0.36	0.36	1.10	0.15
1994	Out of Sample Forecast ⟶				1.34	

Constant	0.48		
Standard Error of *Y* Estimate	0.25		
R-squared	0.85		
Number of observations	17		

	X_1	X_2	X_3
X-Coefficient	1.54	−3.22	3.86
Standard error of *X* coefficient	0.22	1.20	1.21
T-statistic	7.00	−2.68	3.19

Model Data

Here is the data from which the models discussed in Chapter 2 were constructed.

	S&P 500 Return	T-Bill Yield	Aaa Yield	Baa Yield	P/E Ratio	S&P 500 Earnings	CPI	GDP Deflator
1938	0.311				16.3	0.81	−1.9	−1.3
1939	−0.004	0.02	3.01	4.96	11.8	1.06	−1.4	−1.6
1940	−0.098	0.01	2.84	4.75	10.5	1.01	1.0	1.5
1941	−0.116	0.10	2.77	4.33	9.1	0.96	5.0	7.6
1942	0.203	0.33	2.83	4.28	9.5	1.03	10.7	12.3
1943	0.259	0.37	2.73	3.91	12.4	0.94	6.2	7.2
1944	0.198	0.38	2.72	3.61	14.3	0.93	1.7	2.3
1945	0.364	0.38	2.62	3.29	18.1	0.96	2.3	2.6
1946	−0.081	0.38	2.53	3.05	14.4	1.06	8.5	11.8
1947	0.057	0.59	2.61	3.24	9.5	1.61	14.4	11.9
1948	0.055	1.04	2.82	3.47	6.6	2.29	7.8	6.6
1949	0.188	1.10	2.66	3.42	7.2	2.32	−1.0	−0.6
1950	0.317	1.22	2.62	3.24	7.2	2.84	1.0	1.3
1951	0.240	1.55	2.86	3.41	9.7	2.44	7.9	6.9
1952	0.184	1.77	2.96	3.52	11.1	2.40	2.2	2.1
1953	−0.010	1.93	3.20	3.74	9.9	2.51	0.7	1.0
1954	0.526	0.95	2.90	3.51	13.0	2.77	0.5	1.5
1955	0.316	1.75	3.06	3.53	12.6	3.62	−0.4	1.4
1956	0.066	2.66	3.36	3.88	13.7	3.41	1.5	3.4
1957	−0.108	3.27	3.89	4.71	11.9	3.37	3.6	3.7
1958	0.434	1.84	3.79	4.73	19.1	2.89	2.7	2.6
1959	0.120	3.40	4.38	5.05	17.7	3.39	0.8	1.6
1960	0.005	2.93	4.41	5.19	17.8	3.27	1.6	1.6
1961	0.269	2.38	4.35	5.08	22.4	3.19	1.0	1.3
1962	−0.087	2.78	4.33	5.02	17.2	3.67	1.1	1.1
1963	0.228	3.16	4.26	4.86	18.7	4.02	1.2	1.3
1964	0.165	3.55	4.40	4.83	18.6	4.55	1.3	1.6
1965	0.124	3.95	4.49	4.87	17.8	5.19	1.7	1.9
1966	−0.101	4.88	5.13	5.67	14.5	5.55	2.9	2.8
1967	0.240	4.32	5.51	6.23	18.1	5.33	2.9	3.2
1968	0.111	4.34	6.18	6.94	18.0	5.76	4.2	4.0
1969	−0.085	6.68	7.03	7.81	15.9	5.78	5.5	5.0
1970	0.040	6.46	8.04	9.11	18.0	5.13	5.7	5.4
1971	0.143	4.35	7.39	8.56	17.9	5.70	4.4	5.4

	S&P 500 Return	T-Bill Yield	Aaa Yield	Baa Yield	P/E Ratio	S&P 500 Earnings	CPI	GDP Deflator
1972	0.190	4.07	7.21	8.16	18.4	6.42	3.2	4.6
1973	−0.147	7.04	7.44	8.24	11.9	8.16	6.2	6.4
1974	−0.265	7.89	8.57	9.50	7.7	8.89	11.0	8.7
1975	0.372	5.84	8.83	10.61	11.3	7.96	9.1	9.6
1976	0.238	4.99	8.43	9.75	10.8	9.91	5.8	6.3
1977	−0.072	5.26	8.02	8.97	8.7	10.89	6.5	6.9
1978	0.066	7.22	8.73	9.49	7.8	12.33	7.6	7.9
1979	0.184	10.04	9.63	10.69	7.3	14.86	11.3	8.6
1980	0.324	11.51	11.94	13.67	9.2	14.82	13.5	9.5
1981	−0.049	14.03	14.17	16.04	8.1	15.36	10.3	10.0
1982	0.214	10.69	13.79	16.11	11.1	12.64	6.2	6.2
1983	0.225	8.63	12.04	13.55	11.8	14.03	3.2	4.1
1984	0.063	9.58	12.71	14.19	10.1	16.64	4.3	4.4
1985	0.322	7.48	11.37	12.72	14.5	14.61	3.6	3.7
1986	0.185	5.98	9.02	10.39	16.7	14.48	1.9	2.7
1987	0.052	5.82	9.38	10.58	14.1	17.50	3.6	3.2
1988	0.168	6.69	9.71	10.83	11.7	23.76	4.1	3.9
1989	0.315	8.12	9.26	10.18	15.4	22.87	4.8	4.4
1990	−0.032	7.51	9.32	10.36	15.5	21.34	5.4	4.3
1991	0.306	5.42	8.77	9.80	23.4	17.86	4.2	4.1
1992	0.077							

Data Distributors

1. *Barron's*, published weekly by Dow Jones & Co., 200 Liberty Street, New York, NY 10281, contains up-to-date monetary, economic, and financial market data.

2. The New York Federal Reserve, 33 Liberty Street, New York, NY 10045, publishes financial, economic, and monetary data, much of which can be downloaded from its free bulletin board service called Liberty Link.

3. The St. Louis Federal Reserve, Post Office Box 442, St. Louis, MO, 63166, also maintains a free bulletin board service called FRED, which provides current U.S. and international economic and financial data, including daily U.S. interest rates, historical data on money, and business indicators.

4. Ibbotson Associates, 225 North Michigan Avenue, Suite 700, Chicago, IL 60601, publishes *Stocks, Bonds, Bills and Inflation* annually each spring with monthly data going back to 1926. The series in the book are large common stocks (S&P 500), small-company stocks, long-term corporate bonds, long- and intermediate-term U.S. Treasury bonds, U.S. Treasury bills, and inflation (the Consumer Price Index).

5. Pinnacle Data Corp., 460 Trailwood Court, Webster, NY, 14580, distributes monetary and economic indicators, U.S. equity index prices, and data on puts and calls and market breadth. Pinnacle also maintains commodity price and Commitments of (commodity) Traders Report data.

6. UST Securities Corp., 5 Vaughn Drive, CN5209, Princeton, NJ 08543, maintains a comprehensive database of domestic and international equity, fixed income and currency prices and indicators.

ASSET ALLOCATION SOFTWARE VENDORS

1. SciTech International, Inc., 2525 North Elston Avenue, Chicago, IL 60647, publishes a software catalog called *SciTech Software for Science*. The catalog contains econometric, statistical, data analysis and visualization, curve fitting, and forecasting software titles.

2. Computer Handholders, Inc., P.O. Box 59, Arcola, PA 19420, makes *Modern Portfolio Theory Software*, a portfolio optimization package. The program includes five asset allocation models (full covariance, full co-semivariance, lower partial moment heuristic algorithm, single index, and fixed average correlation) in versions that can handle from 25 to 150 assets.

3. Portfolio Software, 14 Lincoln Avenue, Quincy, MA 02170, makes *Asset Allocator*, an inexpensive program that uses the standard mean/variance algorithm for portfolio management.

4. Sponsor-Software Systems, Inc., 860 Fifth Avenue, New York, NY 10021, makes *The Asset Allocation Expert*, with which the user can choose between standard deviation and downside risk as risk measures for optimization. The program can handle symmetrical and asymmetrical asset return distributions as inputs.

5. Wilson Associates International, 7535 East Hampden Avenue, Suite 101, Denver, CO 80231, makes *RAMCAP*, a portfolio optimization program that maintains a database of historical returns for 115 asset classes from 1969 to present. Other asset allocation products come with more extensive data on stocks, mutual and closed-end funds, and variable annuities.

6. Northfield Information Services, Inc., 184 High Street, 5th Floor, Boston, MA 02110, designs and develops asset allocation and portfolio optimization software for institutional clients. The company also provides quantitative

models for both domestic and international equity markets. Northfield's models allow the user to control risk, select desirable securities, construct portfolios, systematically allocate funds across asset classes, and analyze historical performance.

STATISTICAL SOFTWARE VENDORS

1. See the SciTech International, Inc., software catalog reference listed at the top of the previous page.

2. For what it's worth, I use a program called Micro TSP (PC DOS Version 7.0), produced by Quantitative Micro Software, 4521 Campus Drive, Suite 336, Irvine, CA, 92715. The program comes with a user's manual full of examples that are likely to help someone new to econometric modeling get off on the right foot. Since the release of Version 7.0, QMS released a new PC Windows and Macintosh version called Econometric Views, or EViews for short.

3. The *Journal of Business Forecasting* published an article called "A Directory of 66 Packages for Forecasting and Statistical Analysis." The article, which appears in Vol. 8, no. 2 (1992), was written by Aghadazeh and Romal.

4. *The American Statistician*, published by the American Statistical Association, 1429 Duke Street, Alexandria, VA 22314, has a statistical computing section with statistical computing software reviews.

GLOSSARY

Adjusted *R*-squared A second calculation of the *R*-squared measure that takes into consideration the number of predictor variables in a regression model. When predictor variables are added to a model, the *R*-squared always rises, but the adjusted *R*-squared may rise or fall. The adjusted *R*-squared is appropriately used to compare the explanatory power of competing models when the models have different numbers of predictor variables. Also called the *corrected R-squared.*

Adjusted *t*-statistic A *t*-statistic that corrects for the existence of overlapping data, which inflates the normal t-statistic. An inflated *t*-statistic may incorrectly imply that a predictor variable is significant, when in fact it is not. The adjusted *t*-statistic is approximately equal to the reported *t*-statistic divided by the square root of (n_t / n_i), where n_t is the total number of observations, and n_i is the number of independent observations of a linear regression model.

Bid-ask spread The difference between the prices at which an asset can be purchased (the asking price) and sold (the bid price) in a market. The size of the bid-ask spread is an indicator of the cost of trading—markets with narrow spreads tend to be inexpensive to trade, and vice versa.

Call A contract that offers the right, but not the obligation, to buy an asset at a specified price at or before a specified time.

Classical assumptions Assumptions made about a linear regression model that, if satisfied, allow an analyst to make certain conclusions about the regression estimates.

Collinearity An indication of the correlation between two variables. For example, two variables are completely collinear if their correlation is 1. A regression model is said to suffer from collinearity if two of its predictor variables are highly correlated.

Consumer price index An index published monthly by the U.S. Department of Labor indicating the change in price of a basket of goods and services representative of a typical consumer's purchases. The consumer price index is an indicator of price inflation for individuals (as opposed to businesses).

Corrected *R*-squared See *adjusted R-squared.*

Correlation A measure of the tendency, or lack thereof, for two variables such as asset prices to move in the same or opposite direction.

Credit spread See *default premium.*

Durbin-Watson statistic A measure indicating whether regression residuals from adjacent time periods are correlated. The D-W statistic falls between 0 and 4. Values sharply less than 2 indicate that adjacent residuals are positively correlated; a figure sharply greater than 2 indicates negative correlation; a figure approximately equal to 2 indicates that there is no correlation.

Default premium The difference in yield between low- and high-quality bonds. The default premium can also be configured as the ratio of low- and high-quality bond yields.

Deflator A numerical measure designed to distinguish between the current value and quantity of output. When the current value of output is divided by a deflator, it creates an estimate of the quantity of output. A deflator is an indicator of price inflation.

Dividend yield The annual dividend of a stock divided by its current price. For an index of stocks like the S&P 500, the dividend yield is weighted according to each stock's weight in the index.

Earnings-price ratio The ratio of a stock's annual earnings and its price. Sometimes analysts prefer the earnings-price ratio to the price-earnings ratio because in the case of the latter, the denominator can take on positive or negative values or values that are very close to zero, making the variable unruly. Indeed, if earnings equal zero, the price-earnings ratio is undefined whereas the earnings-price ratio is defined.

Error terms See *residuals.*

Ex-ante forecast An out-of-sample forecast in which the actual outcome has not yet occurred.

Ex-post forecast An out-of-sample forecast in which the actual outcome has already occurred.

Forecast An estimate of the mean of an asset's return distribution over some period in the future.

Forecast variable In a regression model, the variable being forecast. Also called the *dependent variable* of a model.

Gross domestic product The current value of goods and services produced within a country.

Holding period return   The return on an asset in decimal form plus one. The holding period return is useful for chaining a series of returns into a single cumulative return. For example, if the return on an asset is 10 percent in period 1 and 7 percent in period 2, then the cumulative return for both periods is

$$(1.10 \times 1.07) - 1 = .177 \text{ or } 17.7\%$$

Implementation costs   The total cost of trading, including commissions and fees, the bid-ask spread, the tendency to move the market, and even the cost of missing trading opportunities.

Influence point   An observation that if removed from a model, causes the explanatory power of the model to fall sharply.

In-sample forecast   A forecast made from an observation included in the data used to estimate a model. See *out-of-sample forecast.*

Least squares   A criterion in which the sum of the squared differences between actual outcomes and in-sample forecasts is minimized.

Linear regression   A statistical technique in which a straight-line relationship between a single variable and one or more other variables is estimated.

Logarithm   Given a base number, the exponent that indicates the power to which the base number is raised to produce a given number. For example, the logarithm of 100 in base 10 is 2 because $10^2 = 100$. Logarithms of base 10 are called common logs and logarithms with a base of the constant e (which equals approximately 2.718) are called natural logs.

Market timing   An investment strategy in which funds allocated to a designated set of assets are adjusted on an ongoing basis in response to changes in forecasts of return, volatility, and correlation of those assets. Also called *tactical asset allocation.*

Multicollinearity   An indication of a linear relationship among three or more variables. A regression model with more than two predictor variables is said to suffer from multicollinearity if there is a strong linear relationship among any three or more of the predictor variables.

Normal distribution   A distribution that approximates the distribution of many random variables. The distribution has a symmetric bell curve shape.

OEX 100   An index of 100 very large-capitalization stocks that trade in the United States. The OEX 100 is a subset of the S&P 500.

Open interest   For derivatives such as options or futures contracts, the number of contracts outstanding at the close of a given trading day.

Outlier   An observation in a regression model in which the in-sample forecast and actual value of the variable are sharply different.

Out-of-sample forecast   A forecast made from an observation not included in the data used to estimate the model. See *in-sample forecast.*

Predictor variable   In a regression model, a variable used to forecast another variable. Also called an *independent variable.*

Price-earnings ratio   The ratio of a stock's price and its annual earnings. Typically, it is considered an indicator of value. The price-earnings ratio can also be computed for an index of stocks, such as the S&P 500 or the Dow Jones Industrial Average. See *earnings-price ratio.*

Proxy   In the context of variables used in statistical models, a proxy is a known variable used as substitute for a variable that is too difficult or impossible to quantify. For example, in modeling agricultural output, an analyst might use average rainfall and the number of sunny days as a proxy for "weather."

Put   A contract that offers the right, but not the obligation, to sell an asset at a specified price at or before a specified time.

Regression   See *linear regression.*

Residuals   For each observation in a model, the difference between the in-sample forecast and the actual value of the forecast variable.

Return   The percent change in the market value of an investment over some period of time, taking into consideration both price changes and any reinvested cash flows, such as interest, dividends, or special distributions. Also called the *total return on an investment.*

R-squared   A measure of the proportion of squared variation of a forecast variable about its mean that is explained by the predictor variable(s) of a model. Also called the *coefficient of determination.*

S&P 500   A capitalization-weighted index of 500 common stocks, it is the most common benchmark for judging the performance of equity portfolio managers.

Serial correlation A variable exhibits serial correlation (also called *autocorrelation*) if there is a relationship between the value of the variable and the value of previous observations of the variable.

Standard deviation Given a random variable X, its standard deviation is calculated by finding

$$(x - x_{mean})^2$$

for each value x. These are the squared differences between each value of x and its mean. The squared differences are summed and divided by n, the number values of the random variable X, to find the average of the squared differences. This average is called the variance of X. The standard deviation of X is the square root of the variance of X.

Standard error of X-coefficient A measure of the precision of an X-coefficient. The smaller the standard error of X-coefficient, the more precise the estimate of the X-coefficient.

Standard error of Y estimate A measure of the explanatory power of a regression estimate. The larger standard error of Y estimate, the poorer the relationship between the predictor and forecast variables.

Stepwise regression An automated technique for selecting predictor variables for a regression model from a group of potential predictor variables.

T-statistic The ratio of an X-coefficient and its standard error. The larger the absolute value of the t-statistic, the more precise the estimate of the X-coefficient.

Tactical asset allocation See *market timing*.

Term premium A measure of the difference in yield between long- and short-term fixed-income instruments. Can also be configured as the ratio of the yields.

Variance See *standard deviation*.

Volatility A measure of the magnitude of an asset's price fluctuations over some period of time.

X-coefficient A regression estimate of how much the forecast variable changes, given a one-unit change in the X-variable.

Yield curve See *term premium*.

ENDNOTES

1. See William Sharpe, "Likely Gains from Market Timing," *Financial Analysts Journal*, March/April 1975, pp. 60–9.

2. See Jess H. Chua and Richard S. Woodward, "Gains from Stock Market Timing," *Monograph Series in Finance and Economics*, Monograph 1986–2, Salomon Brothers Center for the Study of Financial Institutions, Graduate School of Business Administration, New York University.

3. E.F. Fama and K.R. French, "Business Conditions and Expected Returns on Stocks and Bonds," *Journal of Financial Economics* 25 (1989), pp 23–49.

4. John L. Kling and Russell J. Fuller, "Can Regression-Based Models Predict Stock and Bond Returns?" *The Journal of Portfolio Management*, Spring 1994, pp. 56–63.

5. See Stephen M. Stigler, *The History of Statistics* (Cambridge, MA: The Belknap Press of Harvard University Press, 1986).

6. In this book we will use the term *forecast variable* to refer to the variable being forecast and *predictor variable* for a variable being used to make a forecast. In statistics texts, these variables are referred to as *dependent* and *independent*, respectively.

7. For more information on stepwise regression, see John Neter and William Wasserman, *Applied Linear Statistical Models*, 4th ed. (Burr Ridge, IL: Richard D. Irwin, 1996), Chapter 8.

8. Collinearity and the so-called variance inflation factor are discussed in more detail in John Fox, *Regression Diagnostics* (Newbury Park, CA: Sage Publications, 1991), Chapter 3.

9. Readers well acquainted with statistical theory might recall that the standard error of an X-coefficient is actually proportional to the number of observations less the number of degrees of freedom of the regression. There is one degree of freedom for each observation in the regression, but the number is reduced by one for the Y variable and each of the five X variables in the model. Strictly speaking, then, to adjust the t-statistics for the overlapping observations in the model, we should divide the reported t-statistics by the square root of $(360 - 6)/(60 - 6) = 2.56$ instead of the square root of

6, which equals 2.45. As the number of observations increases, the adjustment factor will converge on the square root of six.

10. A few statistical programs will compute the probability that any observed serial correlation is not due to the predictor variables; otherwise Durban and Watson's table appears in most econometric textbooks. For a more thorough review of serial correlation of error terms, see Robert S. Pindyck and Daniel L. Rubinfeld, *Econometric Models and Economic Forecasts*, 3rd ed. (New York: McGraw-Hill, 1991), Chapter 6.

11. The Cochrane-Orcutt or AR(1) procedure is described in Chapter 6 of Pindyck and Rubinfeld (see Note 10).

12. Certainly we can debate whether a model should include a variable that belongs theoretically but is weak empirically. Generally, my take is that a weak variable, by definition, has a coefficient that is not much different from zero. As a result, it will not contribute meaningfully to any forecast. If such a variable still seems promising, it can be left in the model as a reminder that it needs work.

13. Of course, we would not have been limited to using one index or the other as a hedge. Had we been neutral on large versus small stocks, for example, we could have chosen to split the short position 50–50 between the two indexes.

14. Currency forecasting is frustrating because for virtually every set of facts, one can find a theory that says the currency will go down and another that says just the opposite. For a thorough review of the competing models, see Michael R. Rosenberg, *Currency Forecasting: A Guide to Fundamental and Technical Models of Exchange Rate Determination* (Burr Ridge, IL: Irwin Professional Publishers, 1996).

15. Some readers may recognize the scaling of returns according to the correlation of the model forecast as a "Bayesian" adjustment. While this is essentially true, Bayesian methods are normally done using out-of-sample rather than in-sample correlation coefficients.

16. The 0-correlation portfolio still appears to dominate the buy-and-hold strategy by a score of 0.60 to 0.56 due to the use of compound annual returns. If simple mean monthly returns are used and annualized by multiplying by 12, however, the excess return/standard deviation ratios look like this:

	Stocks Buy-and-Hold	Stocks 0-Correlation
Mean return	12.6%	9.2%
Mean T-bill return	4.9	4.9
Mean excess return	7.8	4.3
Standard deviation	16.0	8.9
Ratio excess return/ Standard deviation	0.49	0.48

The difference (0.49 versus 0.48) is due to rounding. We will continue to use compound annual returns, however, because simple means tend to overstate returns, depending on the volatility of the return series. The ratio above using mean excess returns is called the information, or reward-to-variability ratio. This measure and its variants are also called the Sharpe ratio, after William Sharpe. See William F. Sharpe, "The Sharpe Ratio," *The Journal of Portfolio Management*, Fall 1994, pp. 49–58.

17. See Thomas A. Gittings, "Rounding Errors and Index Numbers," *Economic Perspectives*, May/June 1991 (Chicago: Federal Reserve Bank of Chicago), pp. 2–10.

18. For a thoughtful plain-speak article on constructing and testing models, see Carl F. Christ, "Assessing Applied Econometric Results," *Review* 75, no. 2 (March/April 1993) (St. Louis, MO: The Federal Reserve Bank of St. Louis).

19. In order to gauge the potential that hindsight bias lifted simulated returns for the four models proposed in Section 2, readers may find it useful to know that the stock and bond market models were developed in 1989; the large-cap/small-cap and Canadian dollar models, in 1993-94.

20. Some readers will notice that, in order to create forecast probabilities, there is an implicit assumption that the forecast variables are normally distributed. While this is approximately true for six-month excess stock and bond market returns, small-stock relative performance and currencies are both well-known for their tendencies to trend. As a result, the latter two variables may well have distributions that are significantly different from the standard assumptions. There are ways to relax the normality assumption, but they are complex and beyond the scope of this book.

21. A more thorough discussion of asset allocation strategies appears in Edwin J. Elton and Martin J. Gruber, *Modern Portfolio Theory and Investment Analysis*, 5th ed. (New York: John Wiley & Sons, 1995).

22. Some readers may notice that, in order to find each portfolio's utility, we calculate the variance of each portfolio relative to the benchmark portfolio, but we did not calculate the return of each portfolio relative to the benchmark portfolio. Since the expected return of the benchmark portfolio is a constant, subtracting it from the expected return of the active portfolios will not change the order of the portfolio utilities.

23. Readers seeking a fuller discussion of the return and variance on a portfolio of assets are encouraged to see Chapter 2 of Elton and Gruber referenced in Note 21.

24. This so-called mean-variance approach pioneered by Markowitz in the early 1950s assumes that the inputs of expected return, standard deviation, and correlation are perfect. Since they are not perfect, the maximum utility portfolio described here is not the "true" optimal portfolio. It is pretty close, however, since U.S. stocks and bonds have long and relatively stable histories. Methods for finding the true optimal portfolio are mathematically complex. Typically, given the maximum utility portfolio, the true optimal portfolio will be a short distance away in the general direction of the benchmark portfolio. One of the first articles to appear on this subject was by C.B. Barry, "Portfolio Analysis under Uncertain Means, Variances and Covariances," *Journal of Finance* 29, no. 2 (May 1974), pp. 515–22. See also Philippe Jorion, "Bayes-Stein Estimation for Portfolio Analysis," *Journal of Financial and Quantitative Analysis* 21, no. 3 (September 1986), pp. 279–92.

25. When an investor chooses a benchmark portfolio, there is an implied expression of the preferred trade-off between risk and reward. Once this trade-off is established, the issue of how far to wander from the benchmark portfolio can be approached by putting bounds on the standard deviation of the active portfolio relative to the benchmark portfolio. In any case, care has to be taken in differentiating between a short-term tactical change in the asset mix (market timing) and a strategic change of the benchmark portfolio, which typically comes as a result of a change in the investor's economic circumstances such as liabilities, other income, or preference for savings versus consumption.

26. Martin Zweig, *Winning on Wall Street* (New York: Warner Books, 1994), p. 3.

27. Details regarding how to construct several of Zweig's indicators and how to combine them to form a model appear in his book referenced in Note 26 above.

28. Martin Zweig stopped making portfolio recommendations at the close of 1995, but he continues to publish indicator readings in his newsletter and through his telephone hotline service.

29. Edward M. Kerschner, *Asset Allocation/Equity Selection: Explanation of the Models* (New York: Paine Webber, Inc., December 1994).

30. For more commentary on the Leading, Lagging, and Coincident Indicators published by the U.S. Department of Commerce, see Frank J. Fabozzi and Harry I. Greenfield, eds., *The Handbook of Economic and Financial Measures* (Homewood, IL: Dow Jones-Irwin, 1984), Chapter 8.

31. Elaine M. Garzarelli, *Sector Analysis Monthly Monitor* (New York: Garzarelli Capital, Inc., and Zacks Investment Research, October 1995), page 19.

INDEX